I dedicate this book to my Mum and Dad in love and gratitude.

To Matt

Thanks for all that you do for me and MWM.

Blessings to you and your loved ones this Christmas.

In brotherhood

Craig

Index

Introduction 5

Part 1

Chapter 1. Your Inner World 12
Chapter 2. How to come to know yourself – All of yourself 17
Chapter 3. What does it mean to be a man? 22
Chapter 4. Working with Archetypes for self-knowledge 25
Chapter 5. My History and Archetypal Make-up 29
Chapter 6. How to use this book 31

Part 2

Sovereign

Chapter 7. The Heart Sovereign Introduction 34
Chapter 8. The Heart Sovereign Archetype 36
Chapter 9. The Heart Sovereign Speaks 45
Chapter 10. The Sovereign Journey 47
Chapter 11. Into the Underworld 49
Chapter 12. The Crumbling King Archetype 51
Chapter 13. The Crumbling King Speaks 59
Chapter 14. The Tyrant King Archetype 61
Chapter 15. The Tyrant King Speaks 69

Part 3
Magician

Chapter 16. Introduction to the Magician	72
Chapter 17. The Healthy Magician Archetype	76
Chapter 18. The Healthy Magician Speaks	83
Chapter 19. The Manipulator Archetype	85
Chapter 20. The Manipulator Speaks	93
Chapter 21. The Dummy Archetype	94
Chapter 22. The Dummy Speaks	99
Chapter 23. The Safety Officer Archetype	100
Chapter 24. The Safety Officer Speaks	106
Chapter 25. The Predator Archetype	108
Chapter 26. The Self Critic & Predator Speak	116

Part 4
Warrior

Chapter 27. Introduction to the Warrior	120
Chapter 28. The Healthy Warrior Archetype	122
Chapter 29. The Healthy Warrior Speaks	129
Chapter 30. The Bully Archetype	131
Chapter 31. The Bully Speaks	139
Chapter 32. The Pushover Archetype	141
Chapter 33. The Pushover Speaks	143
Chapter 34. Anger and the Warrior	148

Part 5
The Lover

Chapter 35. The Lover Introduction	154
Chapter 36. The Healthy Lover Archetype	159
Chapter 37. The Healthy Lover Speaks	167
Chapter 38. The Wild Lover Archetype	169
Chapter 39. The Wild Lover Speaks	177
Chapter 40. The Lonely Lover Archetype	179
Chapter 41. The Lonely Lover Speaks	186
Chapter 42. The Lover and Sadness	188

Part 6
Next Steps

Chapter 43. Conclusion and next steps	196

Appendix 1. Trauma	197
Appendix 2. Exercises for each Archetype	202

Introduction

This book is aimed at working men who have little time to turn inwards but who want to grow, evolve and mature into their true nature. The men I know, myself included, work hard to keep ourselves growing and thriving. Many of us have responsibilities to hold, love and provide for our families. We live in a challenging world, however, that leaves us few opportunities to attend to ourselves so that we can mature and live at our best.

If we cannot attend to our inner health, we risk living a life dictated to by our early conditioning. If we do not attend to our hurt and wounds, we risk living according to their dictates.

Here you can take the first steps of your Sovereign Journey to know yourself. I have kept my work concise and to the point and set it out so that you can get through the material quickly and easily, particularly the Archetype outlines. My aim is to facilitate your easy recognition of and connection to the various characters who live within you so you can know how you feel, behave and act.

It took me 15 years of exploration to heal myself, so I felt 'good enough' and happy with myself. I had to find my own way as there was no established path in front of me.

I believe that our world needs strong, loving men and that we do not all have 15 years to explore our way into wholeness.

Because of this, I have established the Sovereign's Healing Journey that you can take to wholeness. This Journey will guide you into a mature way of being, living and loving, represented by the Heart Sovereign (King) Archetype.

The work in this book is based on the Jungian Depth Psychology principles of archetypes, shadow and myth.

The Masculine Life Journey

Many of us are familiar with the long-established Hero's Journey. This is the young man's Journey undertaken as he sets out on his adventurous exploration to establish himself in the world. The Hero's Journey has been considered the masculine life journey and the purpose of a man's life, but actually, it is only the Journey for the first half of life. In modern society, we live much longer through our middle and later years. We have a second journey to complete, our Sovereign's Journey to maturity and wholeness.

THE MASCULINE LIFE JOURNEY

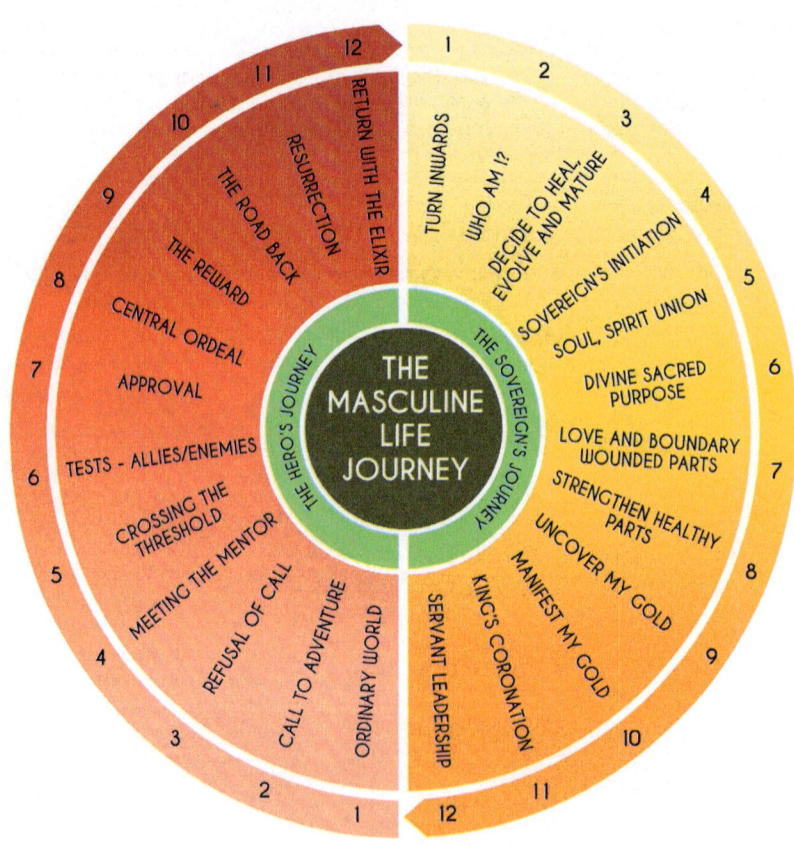

© The Sovereign's Journey

This second Journey is just as adventurous as the Hero's Journey, but it takes place internally rather than in the world.

> "The most adventurous Journey to embark on;
> is the Journey to yourself,
> the most exciting thing to discover; is who you really are,
> the most treasured pieces that you can find; are all the pieces of you,
> the most special portrait you can recognise;
> is the portrait of your soul."
> C JoyBell C

The Hero's Journey is all about forging your way forwards and upwards into life. The Hero is equipped with the conditioned self he adopted as a child and teenager. He brushes his internal wounds and pain under the surface as much as he can and faces into the future to acquit himself. Hopefully, he succeeds and successfully establishes himself in adult life, returning with the elixir he discovered in his Hero's Journey. The Hero's Journey follows an upward arc into life.

The Sovereign's Journey dives downwards into our inner world. This Journey is just as challenging as the Hero's Journey but in a very different way. In the Sovereign's Journey, our King descends into our depths and gets to know and bring to light all our internal characters, including the parts of us that are lost, abandoned, mad, angry, dangerous, sad and frightened. This is soul work, an underworld journey of individuation into our depths where our King learns who we truly are so that he can heal, include, love and integrate our opposites.

> "Your days are numbered.
> Use them to throw open the windows of your soul to the sun.
> If you do not, the sun will soon set, and you with it."
> Marcus Aurelius

In my work with men, I have found that we all want to evolve. We wish to be more successful, lead a more meaningful life, feel more, and contribute to our world. The good news is that all of this is possible, and all of it lies within you. What you are looking for is already here.

I have noticed that many books suggest that we need to be more evolved and "know ourselves" without indicating how this should be done. You will find that this book shows you exactly how to know yourself, inside out.

If it were easy to know yourself, no doubt you would have done that already, as it is far better to be self-aware than it is to be blind to ourselves. Unfortunately, it is not easy. And why should it be? Wise men have encouraged us to undertake this great effort since the beginning of humankind, this inner Journey to "know thyself." When I know myself, I am then in a position to follow the next prompt, "to thine own self be true."

Are you ready for the beautiful, fascinating Journey into yourself?

The Sovereign's Journey is divided into 4 quarters and is led by the King Archetype:

THE SOVEREIGN'S JOURNEY

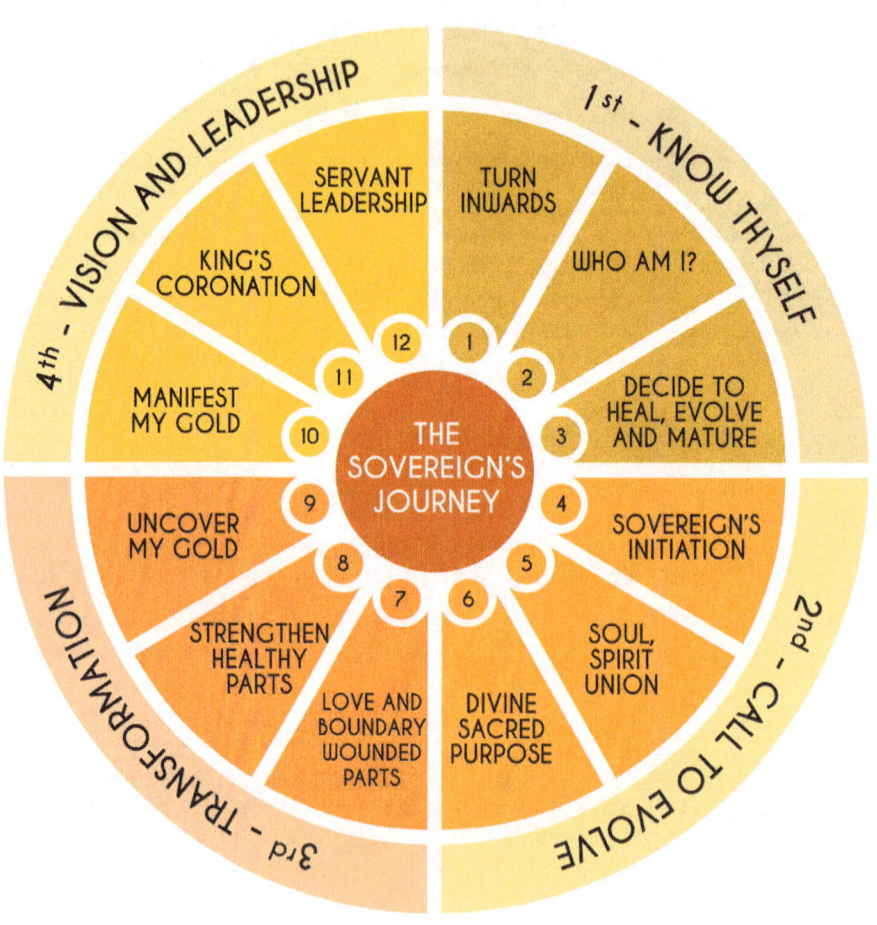

1st Quarter: Know Thyself

If you are reading this book, you probably have already started your investigations into this first quarter. This book is here for you so that you can systematically continue your inner enquiry. In this Quarter, you will lay yourself bare and, in doing so, will lay the groundwork of inner knowing needed to be ready for your Sovereign to mature and integrate you to wholeness.

At the end of our Hero's Journey, something in us changes; maybe a realisation that our Hero's Journey is an unsustainable way of living our life as we get older and our youthful energy wanes. Maybe the parts of ourselves that we have brushed under the carpet in our early Hero's Journey show up more often in our behaviour. Maybe we grow tired of living in automatic and know that something more is needed if we are to be fully alive and connected to the people we love and share our life with. Maybe something goes wrong with our health or in a significant relationship.

At this stage, with the help of your psychologically and shamanically orientated Magician, you can take the opportunity to look openly and honestly at where you are in life, who you are and what you have become. This can be a painful descent into our wounding, adaptive behaviour patterns, trauma and shadow. You are about to dive deeply into your past and how it shapes your present so that you can truly see and acknowledge who you are, warts and all.

2nd Quarter: The Call to Mature

Now that you have some idea of your inner character, it is time to initiate your Sovereign so that your King can guide you down your chosen path to maturity.

It is likely that your internal investigation in the 1st Quarter left you with a strong desire to heal and get clear on how you wish to lead the rest of your life. Like me, I guess you will have learned that you are a product of your childhood conditioning and that you have been hurt and probably wounded in your life journey. Now, as your loving Heart Sovereign, you have an opportunity to heal all you find within and manifest yourself into the world according to your unique design.

The second Quarter of your Sovereign's Journey starts with your King's Initiation. On this weekend, your King will firmly establish himself on your Heart Throne as the guiding and maturing force for your Kingdom. He will then make an intimate connection with his two brother Kings. He will start his long Journey of integration with your Golden Boy and take steps to establish himself as the loving, guiding heart of your Kingdom.

On the second retreat, Soul, Soul and Spirit, your King unifies himself with his allies. He establishes himself as the channel through which love can pour into the world.

Channelling his allies, he crystallises his vision of his particular gifts for the world and clarifies how he will deliver them.

Your King is now ready to build your new world.

3rd Quarter: Transformation

Building on your efforts in the 1st Quarter of your Journey, your Sovereign now systematically makes a relationship with all the parts of you operating in your Magician, Warrior and Lover Archetype. This part of the Journey takes place during Retreats 3, 4, and 5.

At this stage, your King develops a relationship with both your wounded parts and healthy parts. He cares for your hurt and wounded parts, loves them, welcomes and honours their presence. Our King places guidelines and boundaries around how our wounded, particularly our destructive parts, can behave. In time, once these parts have settled into their new way of being, our King will work with them to bring their unique and particular contribution to our Kingdom.

Our Sovereign builds an intimate relationship with all our healthy parts so that he can support and guide them according to our sacred purpose. Partnering with our healthy Magician, Warrior and Lover, he creates the world our Kingly heart most longs for.

Now that our King is in an intimate relationship with all of ourselves, he can get clear on our gold, our gifts, and our particular genius. He searches inside us to unearth our unique talents and particular abilities so that we can contribute them to the world.

4th Quarter: Vision and Leadership

Finally, before he is Crowned, our King reviews our Gold. He gets clear on what vehicles he will use to deliver our particular gifts to our world in a way that has maximum effect.

On your King's Coronation, we will crown your Sovereign in all his grit and glory so that from now on your King is firmly established on your inner Throne and in the driving seat of your life. Your King has now established himself in solid loving leadership. He is now in a place of true elderhood, akin to the Bhoddisatva, and ready to embark on his plan for Servant Leadership.

If your King is ready for this soulful Journey, I stand alongside you.

Let's adventure together.

We have a long journey ahead.

> "The present life of man upon earth, O King, seems to me,
> In comparison with that time which is unknown to us,
> Like the swift flight of a sparrow through the mead-hall,
> Where you sit at supper in winter,
> With your Ealdormen and thanes,
> While the fire blazes in the midst, and the hall is warmed,
> But the wintery storms of rain or snow are raging abroad.
> The sparrow, flying in at one door, and immediately out at another,
> Whilst he is within, is safe from the wintery tempest,
> But after a short space of fair weather,
> He immediately vanishes out of your sight,
> Passing from winter to winter again.
> So this life of man appears for a little while,
> But of what is to follow,
> Or what went before,
> We know nothing at all."
> St Bede.

Part 1

Your Inner World

*"It's your road, and yours alone.
Others may walk it with you,
but no one can walk it for you."*
Rumi

The picture of myself that I present to the world is not the whole picture. Beneath my socially acceptable persona, I have a hidden, darker shadow side that holds all of me that I don't want the world to see. Beneath my accentuated loveable exterior lurks my insecurities, my greed and dominating ambition, my aggression and selfishness.

Even I do not know my complete self. I have inklings of my concealed interior, but I habitually concentrate on playing the role I have constructed to present a front to the world that is socially suitable and brings me what I need. Most of the time, I am not aware I am playing this "presentable" role. I believe this is just "me".

To stay liked and loved, I try to keep my darker side hidden. This takes a lot of energy as these concealed parts of myself hold power and vitality, and they want to "do their stuff". Every aspect of me, the acceptable and the unacceptable, the known and the hidden, wants to live and express itself.

It takes a lot of effort not to be all of myself, especially as I get older and my strength wanes. As I age, I get tired of wearing a mask and performing. When I am exhausted or stressed, control of my dark side slips and I behave in destructive ways. When my old, buried wounds and insecurities are triggered, I freeze, lash out or run away. I blame other people or my circumstances, but somehow, I keep making the same mistakes.

Carl Jung called this hidden side of my character the shadow, all the parts of myself I don't want anyone to see. I hide these aspects of myself from the world and myself if I can. How thick and dense my shadow is depends on how much of myself is hidden there.

Like much of the rest of my psyche, my shadow was primarily formed in my early childhood. I came into life with tremendous energy and primal natural wildness. I did not know what ways of behaving were acceptable and what were not. I freely expressed my aggression. I took against things and people and wanted to hurt them. I was selfish and deviously sought to get what I wanted.

I was also a small, vulnerable child utterly dependent on my parents. They wanted me to behave in a socially acceptable way. I naturally watched out for their disapproval and sought to please them, so I dampened down my energy and reduced the behaviour they discouraged. Teachers and society reinforced this pressure to be a certain way. I learned what parts of myself I needed to restrain so that I could fit in. A portion of who I am moved underground into my shadow. I reduced my intensity by stifling my emotions and dulling my wildness. I adjusted myself to integrate. Parts of myself went underground. Not just my wildness and strong emotions, but also my wounds and pain that I could not address.

How my Shadow Expresses Itself

The unconscious is where it has always been, on the edge of consciousness, intertwined with consciousness, where we do not look or do not want to see.

The unconscious surrounds us. We are immersed in the psyche.

As the alchemists insisted,

the gold of potential lies in the ugly waste of what we have at hand."

James Hillman

All parts of me want to live and express themselves, so it takes a great deal of effort for me to keep my socially unacceptable aspects out of sight. It is hard work only to present my agreeable, pleasant social mask. At times the hidden parts of my character slip out and express themselves.

When this happens, I behave in the following ways:

- I behave improperly, and then I deny my bad behaviour. I ferociously deny my guilt when I am caught out.
- I behave in contradictory ways. I say I am loving, but I hold grudges and agitate against someone I dislike.
- I explode emotionally. Despite my gentle, accommodating front, I have angry outbursts when things go wrong or don't go my way.
- I do something "by accident". I get drunk and aggressively start a fight. I blame my behaviour on the alcohol and do not accept that it was a shadowy part of me that expressed itself when drink loosened my habitual control.
- I "project" my hidden shadow onto others. I get annoyed by their selfishness and aggressive bloody-mindedness, but I only see these qualities in them, not in myself. I despise them for the way they behave and deny that behaviour in myself.
- I don't just project my dark side onto others. I also project my beautiful golden aspects onto others. I see another person as beautiful or as a fantastic leader, but I do not realise that I too have these qualities.
- I am drawn to darkness in my culture. I follow leaders who hate, divide and attack. I am thrilled that this permits me to release my own darkness. I hide in the group and vent in ways my society would usually never allow.
- My shadow shows up particularly strongly in my teenage years and my early twenties.
- I notice my shadow showing up in my dreams.

All the socially acceptable aspects of myself I am so happy about have their corresponding dark opposite. I show the world how much I love while I hide how much I hate. I say I am peaceful, and I hide my violent urges. I try to emphasise my light so that no one notices my dark. I act the saint while hiding my demons.

My hidden personality is not passive and silent. Its many aspects have life and power and demand inclusion and expression. Parts of myself that I deny turn against me and corrode me from within. They show up in my obsessions, the vices that I hide and, in my thoughts, actions, moods and emotions.

It's not easy to know your Shadow

*"And the day came
when the risk to remain tight in a bud
was more painful than the risk it took to blossom."*
Anais Nin

In some ways, it feels easier just to continue to follow my old path of repressing my darker side while appearing to be only loving and kind. I could continue to make excuses when my shadow breaks out, and I do something horrible. I could continue to be blind to much of myself.

It isn't easy to deliberately bring to light the many aspects of myself that I have always kept hidden. To start with, it is difficult to know these aspects as I have kept them locked away for a long time. Parts of who I am have not seen the light of day for years, decades even. Even though I probably don't remember, I hid these aspects deliberately as I bent myself to be socially appropriate and correct. I hid them because I understood that the people around me did not want me to behave in these ways, and I would be shamed and judged if I did. To suddenly about-face and drag hidden aspects of myself out of their underground home is painful and frightening.

Even though it goes contrary to all my conditioning, keeping large portions of myself hidden so that I appear socially acceptable is not wise or healthy. What is called for is for me to walk the path of self-knowledge. I need to delve into my shadow and bring its many aspects to my awareness. I need to know all the parts of myself that I have hidden. This is the pathway to healing and wholeness.

*"Salvation will come to you from the rejected.
Your Sun rises from the muddy swamps."*
C. Jung

Knowing my dark side, I can love and accept these parts of myself rather than hiding and running from them. I can regulate and direct them, and so become more authentic and move from being half a human to being fully human.

In this book, you will experience many different parts of yourself, your healthy, natural whole aspects, and your wounded suffering aspects. You will then have an opportunity that most men long for, an opportunity to see yourself as everyone else sees you, from outside yourself. I expect you have noticed how good you are at seeing dysfunction in others and how they can spot it in you, but you find it more difficult to see in yourself. Now you can see you just like they see you!

This "bringing to light" of parts of yourself is your first effort in this book. That is what self-awareness is. This is how you "know yourself". You will be getting to know many parts of yourself; the "good" and the "bad", the many characters who make up the particular design of your personality.

You will become familiar with and feel more deeply the aspects of yourself you are already aware of, and you will meet and get to know the other half of your character until now hidden in your shadow.

This journey is not just re-joining with your shadow, though. You will also have opportunities to remember your childhood where you were that younger, earlier version of yourself. You will search for and reconnect with who you were before your shadow was forced under the surface. You can reunite with lost and unexpressed parts of yourself and give them home and expression.

Your King will Facilitate your Journey

I will be your guide and friend on your journey, but your exploration will be managed and governed by a particular part of yourself; your King. Your King will get to know all of you and will come into a relationship with all the parts of you he will meet. He will endeavour to accept all parts of you that he knows and loves. He will also attempt to uncover and know all aspects of you he will meet in your shadow. His effort will be to love and integrate all of yourself.

Entering your shadow has a double edge to it. On one side is the pain of reliving the root time or incident that wounded you. It is painful to go back and uncover the times and events in the past that hurt. For me, it was shocking to see how I behave as a result of what happened.

And on the other side is the tremendous relief of finally turning towards deeply hurting, upset parts of yourself and attending to them. When you do this, you turn towards a part of yourself that have been previously banished. You tried to keep these painful parts shut away, out of sight and out of mind, mostly. Turning to these exiled, lonely parts of yourself, you finally recognise and seek to include and heal their suffering.

Your Opportunity to be Whole

*"The original abandonment, the original abuse,
the original horror has some reason and meaning in it.
It is not senseless.
It is not like being run down like a dog on the highway.
Its meaning most often is the development of tremendous strength,
tremendous power, tremendous intuition."*
-Dr. Clarissa Pinkola Estes

Your courage to be all of yourself will bring you a lifetime of blessings. Not only will your King welcome home formerly unwelcome parts, but he will also, in time, once the new relationship has settled in, be able to encourage these parts to bring forward their particular unique gifts. Every wounded part of you has a specific set of skills developed to survive the wound they received. They offer these gifts to their King when he is courageous and caring enough to come for them and bring them home.

All parts of you long for acceptance, love, a home, and an opportunity to contribute to the beautiful human that is you. It is up to your King to facilitate this. It is the power of his love that makes this possible. In his investigation of you, your King explores your Shadows, your unplumbed depths, your primitive instincts, your darkest imaginings, your deepest desires, and your violent, hateful impulses. He sifts through your memories, dreams and longings. He searches for parts of yourself you lost, or had beaten out of you, or had to betray to survive, or had to hide to protect. It is time for your King to bring all of yourself home to your loving, inclusive, healing heart.

At midlife, you are not the same person you were when you started your adult life journey. In your middle age, you are unlikely to want to continue your heroic effort as you did in your 20's, and your 30's, and your 40's. You no longer have the strength, vigour and excess testosterone energy of your youth. As a maturing man, you most likely want to bring more life to your wider world and explore other aspects of yourself that haven't had a chance to live in your hardworking youth.

The same holds true for your inner world. Many aspects of your character have had enough of being in the shadows. Any part of yourself that you ignore and push away ends up turning against you. Out of sight and out of mind, they attend to their murky revenge. They get ready to leap out just at your most stressful, exhausted moment. They look to undermine and derail. They insist on playing their part of you, even when you try to keep them hidden and quiet. This tendency grows as you age and get weaker.

The ignored parts of you find a way to act out in your life, in dramatic destructive incidents, or by slowly leaching through your control. You create the world outside that matches the world you have within, including your shadow side, even if you can't see it. "What me? I'm the nice guy here".

When a shadow part of you jumps into the driving seat, you become that part and act it out. How long it stays there depends on how clever and powerful it is and how much influence it has in your life, conscious or unconscious.

When that part has taken you over, you just run with it and act it out. It is only when you look back, when you are back in your habitual persona, that you realise that your shadow slipped out. You know it is your shadow because you would not choose to behave that way, but you did anyway.

It is not just problematic parts of you that can be in the shadow. Beautiful parts can be there too. These include your ability to feel sad, the strength you need to stand up for yourself, the possibility of being vulnerable, your ability to let love in or love fully.

It is hard to be at home, happy and fully human, when half of yourself is in shadow.

"The privilege of a lifetime is being who you are."

Joseph Campbell

How You Get to Know Yourself – All of Yourself

"And suddenly, you know:
It's time to start something new
and trust the magic of beginnings."
Meister Eckhart

You can use this book to look inwards to get to know yourself extremely well. Knowing who you are is a minimum necessity for every man in this, your one brief life. If you don't know yourself, every effort you make to mature and evolve will always be partial and hampered to some degree.

Within you is a complex, multi-faceted, mysterious inner world. You are conscious of some of yourself, but there are many aspects of you in your "shadow personality" that you are not consciously aware of. These aspects drive your behaviour. They have deep roots, particularly from your childhood and early social conditioning. You can see their effects on your emotions, moods, thoughts and behaviour while you are not aware of their cause.

It is necessary to know yourself so that you understand what is driving your behaviour. With self-awareness, you can change and develop deliberately. You can strengthen and improve the ways you think and act that contribute to your fulfilment. You can limit and redirect the parts of you that struggle or damage your development and happiness. It is impossible to fulfil your potential and grow to your best without improving yourself. You are the base metal of your life, and this base metal needs some work to alchemise you into gold.

Like all humans, you are inhabited by a tendency to evolve, to be the best you can be. You want to progress because you are made that way. You are made to make a meaningful contribution to life. To do this effectively, you must know yourself so you can contribute your gifts without limit.

"Creatures are all striving after their primitive pure nature,
after their supreme perfection."
Eckhart

If you try to resist this tendency, fate and luck will try to direct you there. Maybe your life will stop working, so you have no option other than to fight your way out of the mud. Perhaps you will be subject to a tragedy or painful loss. You may be hurt or become ill so that you can no longer function gracefully.

If you are lucky, you will listen when a kind friend points out a pathway to you. I hope that what you find here is a way forward. I intend to provide you with an evolutionary journey to loving Kingly maturity.

By midlife, your heroic effort to create yourself in the world is well established. Now, hopefully, you have time to go deeper, to make sense of yourself and the life you have lived. Now is a time to get clear about who you are and how you intend to live the rest of your life. You need to turn inwards if you wish to grow. Your wounds prepare the ground for you and call for your attention. They hold aspects of your true power. They have equipped you to bring something particular to the world. Until you face your wounds, this power stays latent.

In time you have lived long enough to see patterns in how you have behaved over the years. You have seen what has worked and what has not worked. You have noticed that the rocks you trip over, again and again, are strikingly similar. Your repeated blunders hurt more each time. You are running out of youthful energy. It's harder to endure messing up. Any part of you that is pretending becomes exhausting to maintain. Self-deception hurts. Where you are inauthentic, you struggle.

> "Owning our story can be hard but not nearly as difficult as
> spending our lives running from it.
> Embracing our vulnerabilities is risky but not nearly as dangerous
> as giving up on love and belonging and joy—
> the experiences that make us the most vulnerable.
> Only when we are brave enough to explore the darkness
> will we discover the infinite power of our light."
>
> Brené Brown

Happily, men have responded to this inbuilt calling to evolve since the beginning of time. They have imprinted the character who undertakes this noble effort into all of our deep unconscious. This part of us is represented by the archetype of the King, who leads us to wise maturity, who builds our heart-centred, spiritually connected, generative essence. Within all of us is a King who is ready to lead us to a healthy, profoundly successful, dynamically joyful life.

On The Sovereign's Journey Retreats

Your King is the ruler of your inner domain. He sets the Vision of your world. He develops your character, which expresses the tone of yourself and your life. You can do much of this self-knowing work in this book.

On the retreats I run your King will undertake the other parts of your Sovereign's Journey by creating a deep mature relationship with each part of yourself. Having established a relationship with each part, your King maintains, monitors, and develops these relationships over your lifetime. Every time your King undertakes one of these processes, you further build and solidify your Kingship.

In this beautiful adventure, as the King, you will build your soulful world by gathering together all the regions of your mind, body, beliefs, behaviour, and feelings. You will draw you together, your ordinary grounded life, and your deep transcendental spirituality. You will endeavour to craft your abundant, fertile Kingdom from a stance of profound, inclusive, honouring and loving blessing.

> "Psychological polytheism is not psychotic dissociation or moral relativity; quite the opposite.
> Repression of multiplicity return in the form of disintegration.
> The heroic ego, trying so hard to get it all together, sets up a condition of psychic
> fragmentation.
> We are so used to valuing integration and unity that any suggestion of multiplicity sends us
> off into extremes. Polytheism, however, means "many", not "any".
> It is not that anything goes, but that the soul has many sources of meaning, direction, and
> value."
>
> Thomas Moore

Your King's aim is to get to know yourself inside out by seeking, watching, cultivating, tending, and including all parts of yourself. It is time to sit in your Sovereignty and get to know all of who you are.

Your Sovereign's intention here is to craft yourself, not into normality and satisfied adjustment, but into a richly elaborate life, deeply and profoundly connected in your heart to your society, to nature, to your family, friends, spirit, and your ancestors.

Your King's first effort is to encourage the best of your Healthy Lover, Warrior and Magician. The healthy version is the middle ground of each archetype.

Your King will also tend to the wounded, troubled, struggling, hurt and hurting parts of each archetype. He will seek to love each injured part, knowing as he does the original wound of each. He will bring understanding, healing, solace, relief and protective inclusive loving. Where necessary, he will formulate boundaries within which these parts of himself will have to operate in future.

Your King will negotiate an agreement with each part. You will record all the agreements your King makes. These recordings will provide you with a record of your negotiated agreement with each part. If a part of you reverts to its old pre-agreement behaviour, you can support that part to return to its negotiated agreement with its King.

> "The appointment with oneself
> also means going back and picking up what was left behind:
> the joie de vivre the untapped talent, the hopes of the child.
> If one could see one's own psyche as a mosaic,
> one would not be able to count, let alone live, all the pieces,
> but each one affirmed heals and rewards the wounded soul...
> Seizing permission to live one's reality is essential at midlife."
> James Hollis

Your Kings effort is to inspire you to blossom according to your particular design and flower according to your unpredictable beauty. You are not trying to solve the puzzle of your life. Instead, you want to lovingly appreciate its many mysteries, the strange blend of light and darkness that is the grand complex poetry of your being.

Your King is seeking to know you by being attentively familiar with the way you are. Your observations have the nature of being richly honouring, as you lovingly nurture and bless. You are seeking to care for yourself, not to cure yourself. You are looking to love and heal the pain of the parts of you that struggle and suffer. You inquire into the illness, the weakness, the remorse, the shame, the depression and the anxiety, seeking their course and origins. You don't want to cut them out, surgically remove them, fix or cure them. You want to observe them to find out why they're calling for your attention. You are searching for the aspects of yourself you have disowned, neglected or pushed out of reach.

> "When our wounds cease to be a source of shame
> and become a source of healing,
> we have become wounded healers.
> Our own experience with loneliness, depression, and fear
> can become a gift.
> Our own bandaged wounds will allow us to listen to others
> with our whole being."
> Henri J M Nouwen.

Your Sovereign seeks to give each inhabitant of your Kingdom, each archetype operating within, each internal character, its authentic voice. Your King aims to lovingly appreciate each one, welcome them all, and create a safe, honoured space for each in his Kingdom. Now is the time for your King to encourage forward your previously rejected parts, your 'problem' parts, your lost and split off parts, your challenging parts, your collapsed parts. Your King doesn't judge, shy away from, reject, or moralise about these parts. He fearlessly includes all your oddities, your deviances, your quirks, your shadow tendencies, all the strange landscapes of your being.

You are getting to know your unique character. Ongoing loving care is your intention. You are trying to give your steadfast attention, to watch and listen, and search the mysteries that lie within you. Your King seeks to sympathise with your suffering, digest your problems into opportunities for depth and find beauty within your beast.

> "Joy is the happiness of love
> – love aware of its own inner happiness.
> Pleasure comes from without,
> and joy comes from within,
> and it is, therefore,
> within reach of everyone in the world."
> Fulton Sheen

As the King, you have power in your observation. You look inwards, into your unconscious, sensing and imagining, lovingly enticing parts of yourself out of ignored darkness. You draw in the parched, lonely parts to drink at the healing grail of your heart. Your inner knowing and caretaking will never end, and each seeming ending is just another beginning. Your investigation will take the form of a circle. It will rotate so that you can orbit with curiosity over the material of your psyche, looking again and again at the multi-layered deep mythical themes of your Kingdom.

Your profound interest in your inner world is your way of loving your inner self. You are not seeking a logical understanding, but rather to patiently and carefully embrace all the many complicated multi-faceted aspects of yourself. If you do not do this as you get older, you concretise into your habits. You get older and weaker as you age. Unless you take yourself in hand, your automatic operating system increasingly takes over, so you are run by the beliefs and behaviours established in childhood.

> "Without self-knowledge,
> without understanding the working and functions of his machine,
> man cannot be free.
> He cannot govern himself,
> and he will always remain a slave."
> G.I. Gurdjieff

As you will find out, when you proceed down your King's Path, your world changes as your King seats himself on your inner heart throne. Your life starts to work, as you always wished it would. You move from potential into manifestation. Doors open, opportunities beckon, your life makes sense, and you naturally, effortlessly, happily fulfil your destiny.

> *"The heart is a vital organ, but also a great territory.*
> *The heart is where true imagination resides.*
> *Courage is a heart word that derives from the Latin cor;*
> *it refers to the core of one's deepest feelings and innermost thoughts.*
> *For the heart harbours thoughts and dreams as well as feelings and emotions.*
> *The heart can be mined for enduring courage and living imagination;*
> *courage required to become oneself.*
> *Our way of loving and healing is seeded within us,*
> *yet it takes more than one breakthrough to reach the inner treasure.*
> *A long road made of longing and self-discovery is required*
> *in order to re-open the heart and reveal the gold within it.*
> *"what the heart loves is the cure."*
> *Life is the ailment and what we love provides the cure for what ails us."*
> Michael Meade

This is a time to stand back from your life, take some perspective on yourself. It will be helpful for you to get into the habit of observing yourself and your life. Notice how you think. Observe your thoughts. Watch your behaviour. Be with your feelings. Watch out for patterns in the way you live and see if you can work out their root causes. Dwell on your past.

> *"I don't aspire to be a good man,*
> *I aspire to be a whole man."*
> C.G. Jung

Blessings on your journey!

What does it mean to be a Man?

The Patriarchal Model of Masculinity

This way of being a man, adhered to by my father, grandfather, and the men before them, encouraged men to be brave and strong. This model worked for men who led hard, demanding lives of toil, danger, and struggle. These men ruled empires, fought wars, and lived tough working lives.

In this model, men were conditioned to be resilient and unemotional. They were expected to hold their own, on their own. A hard man never backed down and did not ask for help. Anger was allowed and encouraged, but men could never show sadness or fear.

> "There have been so many times
> I have seen a man wanting to weep
> but instead beat his heart until it was unconscious."
> Nayyirah Waheed

This model helped men survive and thrive in challenging times. When life was difficult and dangerous, men needed to dominate their fear and weakness. They had no time and place for sadness and mourning. Men crushed the gentler sides of themselves to keep going. They did what was required to make a living and support themselves and their families. Many men put aside their personal happiness to do what had to be done.

There are many drawbacks to this patriarchal way of being a man. The main disadvantage of this approach is that it is much more like the Tyrant King and the Bullying Too Much Warrior than it is like the Heart King and the Steadfast Warrior. Without softer emotions, men are stoical and emotionally armoured. They take pride in never being vulnerable. They put little value in the ability to relate emotionally and are uninterested in emotional expression or emotional literacy. They hide their hurt and wounding and try to ignore and get over their pain without feeling or discussing it. Hard men believe that they should always be able to cope and hold it together without help. If a man struggles, he hides it.

This old way of being a man leaves many men leading lives of "quiet desperation". They feel that they have little choice around how to be a man. Many men suffer tremendously trying to function in this hard masculine way.

> "Emotional neglect lays the groundwork for the emotional numbing
> that helps boys feel better about being cut off.
> Eruptions of rage in boys are most often deemed normal,
> explained by the age-old justification for adolescent patriarchal misbehaviour,
> "Boys will be boys."
> Patriarchy both creates the rage in boys and then contains it for later use,
> making it a resource to exploit later on as boys become men.
> As a national product, this rage can be garnered to further imperialism,
> hatred and oppression of women and men globally.
> This rage is needed if boys are to become men willing
> to travel around the world to fight wars
> without ever demanding that other ways
> of solving conflict can be found."
> Bell Hooks

This patriarchal way of being male that we have inherited has had a considerable effect on the world and on individual men's lives. Men are expected to be aggressive, driven, ambitious and competitive. They are taught to be invincible and invulnerable and to want to conquer themselves and the world. While this approach may have helped get things done, it created a world where men could be abusive, controlling and domineering.

Cold, hard, emotionally distant men create a very harsh world for all of humanity. Strong unfeeling men keep others in their place. They try to control the feminine and to dominate and use the earth. They rule the world rationally to create a male environment of status, achievement, work, conquest and wealth, where the gentler loving sides of life are excluded and rejected. This approach has a hugely destructive effect on the earth. It also damages women, children and men themselves. Men who cut off whole areas of their humanity are not happy or fulfilled. They struggle to live deeply connected loving relationships or to be close to their children. All of us have paid a high price for living like this.

Men Start to Change

"We weren't born distrusting and fearing ourselves.
That was part of our taming.
We were taught to believe that who we are in our natural state is bad and dangerous.
They convinced us to be afraid of ourselves.
So we do not honour our own bodies, curiosity, hunger,
judgment, experience, or ambition.
Instead, we lock away our true selves.
Women who are best at this disappearing act earn the highest praise:
She is so selfless.
Can you imagine?
The epitome of womanhood is to lose one's self completely.
That is the end goal of every patriarchal culture.
Because a very effective way to control women
is to convince women to control themselves."
Glennon Doyle

Over the last 120 years, women have questioned the patriarchal model's dominance and their position in it. They were determined to define their feminine world and bring to light the controlling dark underbelly of masculine power. They formed a women's movement, which showed men that another way of being was possible, even preferable. Men started to understand that this harsh patriarchal way of being a man was damaging for the earth, women, children, and men.

Women stood up against male sexual manipulation, control and abuse. Men have slowly incorporated a more feminine outlook and turned to the feminine for inspiration. Following the example of women's groups, men started gathering together to turn inwards to understand themselves better. They were looking to bring to life a more profound, more inclusive way of being male. This internal investigation has led men to become more thoughtful and gentle, more nourishing and nurturing. Gradually men created a new model of being a man who was much more emotional and sensitive.

Men turned away from the old harsh model of masculinity and embraced being gentler, more feeling, and more connected. This brought its own difficulties as Robert Bly states:

"Lovely, valuable people – not interested in harming the earth or starting wars. But many of these men are not happy. You quickly notice the lack of energy in them. They are life-preserving, but not exactly life-giving. Ironically you often see these men with strong women who positively radiate …"

Men who embraced this gentler way of being seemed to lose their core strength and dynamism. They became passive and directionless, without fire and purpose.

Men have had to respond to a profound change in their place in the Western world. The economy has changed so that many traditionally male jobs, particularly in manufacturing, have disappeared. There has been a shift towards a service and information economy.

While men experienced these changes, women found their power and their voice. They moved out of the home into the marketplace and now compete for work with men. Men are mostly no longer able to position themselves as the primary provider in many families.

It became clear to men that they had to evolve this old fashioned, patriarchal way of being a man. They needed to step away from the old destructive masculine model without losing the best that good men can bring to the world. Trying not to be dangerous and abusive, men gave up their dynamic strength and their passionate, adventurous generative and creative power. They swung so far into being gentle that they lost much of their masculine drive and effectiveness. Veering away from the old abusive 'bad' masculine ways, they tried to be "good" men and in turn found that they were again not whole. They moved from shutting down gentleness in men to shutting down power and masculine dynamism.

Now men are searching for a way to be whole. Men are looking for a way to keep their beautiful creative power and effectiveness while also being emotionally literate and compassionately connected. Men need a new model of being a beautiful, fully alive man. Men still want to provide and be successful in the working world while also being active in their homes as equal loving partners and involved caring fathers.

In this book, I offer you a new way of being a man.

"From the standpoint of daily life, however, there is one thing we do know: that we are here for the sake of each other –
above all for those upon whose smile and well-being our own happiness depends,
and also for the countless unknown souls with whose fate we are connected by a bond of sympathy.
Many times a day I realize how much my own outer and inner life is built upon the labours of my fellow men,
both living and dead,
and how earnestly I must exert myself
in order to give in return as much as I have received."
Albert Einstein

Working with Archetypes for Self-knowledge

*"Until you make the unconscious conscious,
it will direct your life, and you will call it fate."*
CG Jung

As explained previously, a part of our journey to authentic happiness requires us to know ourselves well.

How can this be done? Along with other men who have studied masculine development, I propose using archetypes as a mirror in which we men can better understand ourselves.

What are Archetypes?

Many have noticed since the beginning of time that humans tend to conduct themselves in particular ways.

Carl G Jung called these common behaviours archetypes, or "first patterns", the basic blueprints of human drives and qualities that we all share, "a universal and recurring image, pattern, or motif representing a typical human experience." Universal archetypes include the "hero", the "victim", and the "tyrant". The archetype's name summarises its behaviours, so we instantly know the characteristics of the person exhibiting the archetype.

Different people and even different societies exhibit these archetypal patterns to varying degrees. There are many different archetypes. Each has its particular character, way of behaving, beliefs, ways of thinking, actions, values and emotions. They originate from roles, such as that of the Father, or events, such as Death.

Since archetypes are linked to our instinct and our spirit, they are inherited as much as developed. They are charged with intensity and work automatically in our subconscious. Since the beginning of humanity, they have existed as typical situations in life and are engraved in our universal psyche through endless repetition. New archetypes are being created all the time as society progresses. Examples include aliens, Santa Claus, etc.

How do Archetypes work in us?

Because they are in our subconscious, we are not aware of them even as we live them out. As children, we developed our own personal archetypes. We also inherited a collective unconscious, the archetypal ways of being human embedded in our being and common to all humans. Jung calls this "a second psychic system of a collective, universal, and impersonal nature that is identical in all individuals." This underground system within us is full of ancient and familiar archetypes. Each step into life within us when we need them. Each carries within its being its charge and power, and this magnetism comes available to us as the archetype comes alive in us.

Archetypes that live in this collective unconscious can easily be seen in myths and stories, which work with a deep layer in our psyche. The Villain, the Bully, the Addict, and many more are all in our inherited collective subconscious.

Most of us tend to think of ourselves as unique individuals, and we certainly are, but we also contain these drives, patterns, and qualities common to all humans. We each express them in our own particular way. When we study archetypes, we notice those that live in us, and we see how we exhibit and express them in our behaviour.

> *"Be honest with yourself.
> When you are honest with yourself,
> you find the road to inner peace."*
> Paramahansa Yogananda

Working with These Archetypes

Archetypes are very useful as they show particular behaviour patterns. As individuals, if we know the behaviours associated with certain archetypes, we can look at ourselves to acknowledge how we behave in these archetypal ways.

Four particular archetypes – the Lover, the Warrior, the Magician, and the King – were identified by Robert Moore and Douglas Gillette in the 1990s as being present in all human beings. They found this to be true for societies across the world. They saw that the behaviours of these four archetypes, in particular, demonstrate aspects of masculine life that, taken together in their healthy form, show us what it is like to be a well-rounded, mature, high functioning man.

When we look at each of these archetypes in their healthy, well-adjusted functioning, we see a model of behaviour against which we can measure and assess ourselves. They give us a vision and an example of how to behave in each of their archetypal ways.

As typical humans, the healthy behaviours of each archetype come naturally to us. Sadly, we may have found that as children, we faced disapproval and punishment when we behaved in the healthy ways of a particular archetype.

We were then wounded in our healthy functioning so that we learned to act in a wounded way in a particular archetype. When we lost access to the healthy form, we either suppressed that archetype, so it functioned at a low level, or we defiantly exaggerated it. When we exaggerated it, our behaviour demonstrated an amplified model of the archetype.

All of this will become much clearer when we look at the individual archetypes in detail.

Archetypes as an Internal Map

In the coming chapters, you will be able to get to know yourself by looking in the mirror of these archetypes, which present an internal map of the masculine. Seeing how these archetypal characters behave, you will appreciate who you are, both in your healthy and your unhealthy behaviours.

When you seek to understand yourself in the mirror of the archetypes, you take the first step of your evolution, to appreciate and understand who you are. Once you know yourself, you can consciously evolve. If you recognise and accept your dysfunctional behaviour, you can do something about it. Without self-investigation, you will never be able to get better at being yourself.

> *"If you want to awaken all of humanity, then awaken all of yourself,
> if you want to eliminate the suffering in the world,
> then eliminate all that is dark and negative in yourself.
> Truly, the greatest gift you have to give is that of your own self-transformation."*
> Lao Tzu

This journey into self-discovery using these four archetypes is not an easy one. To see how many aspects of our behaviour show up in each archetype's unhealthy wounded form can be painful, humbling and distressing. It takes courage to acknowledge how much of our conduct comes from unconscious wounding. It takes guts to bring ourselves to the light of conscious understanding. Yet the journey is worth it. Authenticity, freedom, joy and happiness lie at hand. To know yourself means to be free to be yourself.

Three Aspects to Each Archetype

Each archetype has three aspects.

First, we look at how a man behaves when he exhibits the naturally healthy behaviours of the archetype.

Next, we look at how a man can be wounded in the archetype and how this wound leads him to act in ways that are too much of the archetype, or too little.

How You will Work with Each Archetype

> *"The ingredients of both darkness and light are equally present in all of us."*
> Elizabeth Gilbert

Some men, especially if they are struggling to hold themselves together, find this process of dividing the individual into their parts somewhat challenging. It is a bit odd but try to bear with it as it helps us see the different aspects of ourselves more clearly if we sift ourselves into separate parts. We are then able to see how we act and behave in detail in each archetype. It is much more challenging to do this if we take male behaviour for man as a whole.

> *"Whose permission are we waiting for to enter that 'uncertain ground'*
> *where the voice of our wild history can be heard?*
> *How long is it going to take to acknowledge*
> *that there is indeed a menagerie within each of us...*
> *a wolf, a hyena, a lion...a wild man and a wild woman?"*
> Ian McCallum

You are seeking as complete a picture of yourself as possible. You are particularly looking for how you have been conditioned to behave in specific ways. You are attempting to unearth the parts of yourself that you do not fully understand or accept. To facilitate this investigation, you can consider the following questions before you have a look at the archetypes:

- What about my earlier life have I suppressed or forgotten?
- What about myself have I denied and put out of sight?
- Where am I constrained and bound by fear, adaption and conventions?
- Where am I keeping myself safe and small?
- Where am I dependent on comfort or on others?
- Where am I lethargic, asleep, numb and unfeeling?
- Where do I control, limit myself, or comply?
- Where do I avoid, not show up, and not take full responsibility for myself?
- Where do I compulsively and repetitively take myself down the same dead-end?
- Where am I separated from my natural, instinctual self?
- How do I attack myself and the world?

Be Gentle with Yourself

I struggled when I realised how much of my behaviour was unhealthy. This self-investigation process is not easy, mainly because actions that show up in their harmful form are usually based on childhood wounds. When I recognise my unwholesome behaviour, I also uncover the wound that generated it. This is doubly painful. I bless your courage to do this work.

> "Short cuts in philosophy do not exist.
> But if they did, the wise man would choose the longer road.
> He would choose it because of the adventures along its way,
> adventures in the mystic processes of becoming.
> Do not grudge the years and the lives which stretch out ahead.
> These are not merely periods of trial and tribulation.
> They are adventures in the mystery of the soul."
> Manly P. Hall

Now is the time to open up to all of who you are. It is time to notice and appreciate who you are without judgment. While it may be painful for you to acknowledge the truth of yourself at times, encourage your King to try as best you can to sit and be with all of yourself. In particular, this is the time to suspend any criticisms you have about yourself, and especially any shame you feel about who you are.

Shame and self-criticism are usually pretty entrenched, but it will help you try to suppress these at this time so you can honestly know yourself. Your effort here is to encourage yourself out of the shadows. To do this effectively, it is essential to welcome all of who you are, the good and the bad. If your King does not embrace an element of yourself but judges and criticises that aspect, then this shamed part of you will tend to hide again and become inaccessible for healing.

Be gentle with yourself. Bring your Kingly love for yourself to the fore.

Each of the healthy archetypes is divided into three particular sections.

1. The first section shows the healthy **behaviours** of that archetype.
2. The second section shows the particular **skills** of that archetype, those aspects of life in which he is exceptionally skilled.
3. The third section lists the archetype's innate **gifts**, those aspects of life that the archetype is brilliant at.

When you look at the archetype's wounded aspects, I have listed the behaviours that demonstrate too much of an archetype and too little.

> "The healing process is best described as a spiral.
> Survivors go through the stages once, sometimes many times;
> sometimes in one order, sometimes in another.
> Each time they hit a stage again, they move up the spiral:
> they can integrate new information and a broader range of feelings,
> utilise more resources, take better care of themselves,
> and make deeper changes."
> Laura Hough

My History and Archetypal Make-Up

I am encouraging you to know yourself and know your archetypal make-up, so it seems that I should demonstrate my own as an example.

I grew up in Africa. Surrounded by virgin bush, I had a wild free adventurous childhood until the age of nine when, with my family, I became embroiled in the Rhodesian (now Zimbabwe) Civil War. From the ages of nine to fourteen, I lived in danger of being attacked and killed.

My experience of being trained and armed to protect my family had a strong effect on my archetypal make-up.

I was often afraid but realised that fear was pointless as it did not stop anything terrible from happening. While we were never attacked, awful things happened to people around me, so from a young age, I understood that being afraid and careful would not keep me safe. I learned that the only thing I could do was to be ready to fight at any time.

As a result, I have lived a life of Too Much Warrior. In the face of any difficulty, I lean into Too Much Warrior. I have always used work as my way of powering myself out of problems. I have also been extremely angry. I never showed this physically with people but would explode in anger over minor frustrations and smash things up. I would punch walls and destroy my possessions. I used my anger to work harder and keep going even when I was exhausted.

In the environment I grew up in, boys were encouraged to be tough and not show any softer emotions. I attended a small local school where children of all ages were educated in the same room by one teacher. When the girl I sat next to in class was killed, with all her family, the school was disbanded, and all children were sent to boarding school, so we were safer in the term time. At boarding school, we were beaten relentlessly. It was social suicide to cry or show any form of weakness, so we all clamped down on any expression of sadness. I shut down my gentler Lover nature and lost the ability to cry. I hid my sadness from others and myself.

I have lived as Too Little Lover all my life. I have only accessed my sadness in the last few years and gradually allowed it to flow. While I love being around people socially, I have found socialising hard work, so I have looked for opportunities to disengage. I need a lot of time on my own to stay balanced.

I would never be vulnerable. I believed that I was not loveable and that I could not love properly. It has taken me a long time to soften into my gentle Lover. I kept myself half available in love relationships and made sure that I always had a way out. I entered relationships with partners who were also not available. I suffered from relationship breakdown again and again.

In Magician, I had very little access to my safe-keeping Safety Officer aspect. When a new opportunity presented itself, I would charge ahead in Warrior with little planning and no assessment of possible risks or problems. I would soon bump into difficulty and had to rely on my Warrior's extra effort to sort the situation out.

Another aspect of my Magician was my belief that I am dark and that there is something fundamentally wrong with me. As a child in the war, I felt hate and darkness surrounding me. I knew I was being hunted and that people wanted to kill me. For many years, I had extremely violent nightmares. I came to believe that my early exposure to conflict had damaged me and that I was dark and violent, maybe even evil.

The part of me that held this violent trauma was my Predator. You will meet this part when you reach the Magician section. My Predator is hard to spot because he will only act out when he has an excuse to do so. He is not like my Bully Warrior, who will just steam in. My Predator makes sure he has 'permission' to act out. This gives him 'cover' within which he can predate.

That permission looks like this:

> "I'm protecting us from evil.
> He's dangerous and must be stopped/wised up.
> I'm doing this for all of us.
> He's terrible, and everyone needs to know it.
> I'm right; he is wrong."

Feeling justified, my Predator steams in.

I know it's my Predator because I'm too excited, it's too important, I'm acting too fast without checking what I am doing, I don't care about the consequences. My words/actions have a hard edge to them and an undercurrent of punishing. My words don't match what I'm doing (I am saying I love you, but it feels more like I'm sticking a knife in your back).

My Predator is trying to show that he is good while he profoundly believes he is bad. And he is bad, though not all bad. He stepped into being when I was a child to make me strong enough to survive in perilous circumstances. He took in the darkness attacking him, and incorporated it and turned it back outwards.

As for my King, I tried for many years to bring this archetype alive within myself. I did not understand then that, while we all have the model of the archetypal King within, this aspect of ourselves needs to be deliberately constructed. Our King doesn't just burst into being fully-fledged! My King has only become solid and central in my life once I undertook the processes in this book that bring him alive as the central maturing, evolving, holding and loving force within. Before I bought my Healthy King alive my prime King was my Tyrant, my Too Much King. This part of me is overpowering, uncaring, narcissistic, and hard hearted.

As you can see, before my Loving King evolved me, I mostly functioned out of wound.

> "You become. It takes a long time.
> That's why it doesn't happen often to people who break easily,
> or have sharp edges, or who have to be carefully kept.
> Generally, by the time you are Real, most of your hair has been loved off,
> and your eyes drop out and you get loose in your joints and very shabby.
> But these things don't matter at all,
> because once you are Real, you can't be ugly,
> except to people who don't understand."
>
> Margery Williams Bianco – The Velveteen Rabbit

How to Use this Book

The 'to do' part of this book!

Overview

In this book, you will see outlines of lots of different archetypes, internal characters who we all have.

This book has dual aims:
1. To grow your King as the leader and mediator of your Inner World.
2. To 'know thyself'. In each process, you will get to know a part of yourself extremely well.

In this book there is a detailed overview of each archetypal part of ourselves, as well as some examples of various men's expression of these parts.

So, for each of the archetypal parts you are looking to get to know how the particular part functions in you.

You will spend time getting familiar with the archetypal part of yourself you are seeking to know. You can do this by reading through the outline of the archetypal part provided in each section and by reading examples of other men's expressions of these parts. I find that these provide a remarkably grounded living sense of the archetype.

Take as much time as you want to get to know this part of yourself. I have tried to illuminate and demonstrate each part by showing how it typically thinks and behaves. This way, you can look at your own thinking and behaviour in the mirror of this archetype.

The archetypal outline I have provided is only a starting point for your investigation. You can use this outline to help you get a taste of the thoughts, patterns, beliefs, and behaviours of each archetype. Hopefully, as you go through the outline, you will also notice how you behave in ways that belong to the archetype that are not listed here.

Write down the ways you behave in each archetype. These notes will provide a foundation for an appreciation of yourself as the archetype.

The Different Parts of yourself that you will get to know

Every part of you has a deep inner longing to be seen, welcomed and loved by you, their King. Your loving, compassionate attention is pure bliss, a healing balm bringing peace, stillness, harmony, cooperation and self-acceptance. You will be getting to know your Healthy parts, and your wounded dysfunctional parts.

Child and Teenage Parts

As you will see when you come to the outline of these parts of you, none of us had perfect parents, and none of us had an ideal childhood.

We all struggled at times as children. We had to fit into our childhood world to thrive. We did not have agency and sovereignty, and all power was held by our parents, by our caregivers, and by authority figures.

It may seem strange at first, but your child still lives in you. The pain of where you were mistreated still lives in you, and your reaction to this pain is still very much alive.

For example, if my mother was critical of me when I grew up, I find myself very reactive when my partner gives me feedback. I take her constructive comments as criticism, and I attack angrily, go numb and absent myself.

My adverse childhood experiences live in me as toxic, disorderly thoughts and reactions as an adult.

My inner child calls for his King's loving healing attention to know and heal him so that he can settle and stop his disordered reactions. King, you are the only person in the world who knows the struggle and pain held in your boy and your teenager. You hold the key to their healing in your loving Royal heart. If you attend my Retreats, you will have many opportunities to offer healing to your inner boy, and the many other parts of yourself.

Part 2

The King

Starting your Journey

Your internal investigation starts with your Healthy Sovereign, your Ideal King. Your King holds a unique position in your archetypes as he functions as the consummate facilitator and conductor of your maturing world.

Your King holds your consciousness. He is conscious of himself and conscious of the many parts of your world and how they all behave.

Your King is your still, aware centre, the fertile authority of your existence. As the dignified King, you see and know all that happens within yourself. As the seat of Kingly consciousness, you notice and acknowledge your thoughts, believe in and direct your actions and feel your emotions knowing you are not them. Your King is your true home, behind all, just watching, the seat of your Self, deep within.

Your King's job is to know himself/yourself inside out. He/you need to know how you respond to events in the world and with which emotions. Your effort is to stay present as your King, separate from what is happening, so you can remain in the driving seat of consciousness and not become the emotion or the part that is reacting. You stay as the witness and don't get sucked into the action. Only then, as Kingly awareness, can you minister to the part of yourself that need your attention. You cannot do this if you become the archetypal part.

By staying aware and open, your King can remain fully energised. Your energy rises from deep within your inner Soul, as Chi, or Spirit energy. Your life energy is endless, and it flows from deep within. As the King, you are responsible for making sure that you keep your sacred fire blazing as you restore, heal, include and recharge your Kingdom. Your great effort is to pull all parts of yourself into the Kingdom of your heart where your beautiful life-fulfilling energy flows.

If you close your heart to any part of yourself or any part of your life, then you restrict your healing and keep the blockage in place. If you close off to any part of yourself, you leave that part excluded in darkness. You limit and reduce the flow of light and love in your world.

Every part of you that you get to know builds your King's essence and presence. Your King will lead you into mature individuality as the part of you that holds all the other parts. Each time you get to know a part you get stronger and more clearly defined. Each time you know, love and include, you bring more love, acceptance, peace and dynamic energy into your system.

Your mature self-knowing King is the pinnacle of your masculine humanity, and living this archetype brings you a beautiful self-fulfilled life. As the King, you can spread love, abundance and blessings to all in your domain.

Feel into the energetic field of your Healthy King. This archetype has powerful energy and lives in all of us as the hope and dream of humanity. Your King is your enlightened Ruler who brings grace to all you do and loves and protects all in your Kingdom.

Take time to read through the healthy King's behaviours and notice where you behave like this archetype. Notice which you recognise in yourself. Take time with your perusal. Tap into the energetic field of this Sovereign archetype. Feel into him inside yourself. As you identify aspects of yourself in the outline you are reading, notice how this archetype plays out in your life.

In what other ways does this Healthy King show up in your thoughts and actions? This list of behaviours is here for you as a starting point, so you can recognise the Healthy King. In what other ways, not listed here, do you act as a Healthy King?

Remember that this outline is aspirational. No one is as beautiful and powerful as this King! The outline is here to bring to light the many aspects and characteristics of the Healthy King so you know what you are looking for in yourself. Whatever you find, you can build on that.

If your reaction to this King is, "I can never be that", your Crumbling King is speaking.

If your reaction is "What a weak wanker, I am much better than him", your Tyrant is speaking.

As you read about the Healthy King Archetype, write down the aspects of the good King which you recognise as existing in you. Feel into the many other ways your true King plays out in you so you can feel and know them and write them down. Spend what time you need with your King to get a good picture of how you live as him.

The Sovereign Archetype

Letter from Albert Einstein to his daughter Leiserl.

> "There is an extremely powerful force that, so far, science has not found a formal explanation to.
>
> It is a force that includes and governs all others, and is even behind any phenomenon operating in the universe and has not yet been identified by us.
>
> This universal force is love.
>
> When scientists looked for a unified theory of the universe they forgot the most powerful unseen force.
>
> Love is Light, that enlightens those who give and receive it.
>
> Love is gravity, because it makes some people feel attracted to others.
>
> Love is power, because it multiplies the best we have, and allows humanity not to be extinguished in their blind selfishness.
>
> Love unfolds and reveals. For love we live and die,
>
> Love is God and God is Love."

- I am the guiding **King at the Centre of my World,** and my generative influence radiates across my Kingdom.
- I am responsible for my blossoming. I accept the risk of flowering. I steward my rise out of potential into blessed wholeness. I manifest my light and my King's Calling into a life of service and graceful abundance.
- I am the **ruler and leader** of my progressive world. I hold my big picture together, my miraculous Kingdom, even through incoherent chaos, paralyzing fear, and ignominious drama. I lead with dignity, possibility and warm-hearted compassion. I am concerned for and steward my realm.
- I take total responsibility for everything that happens in my Kingdom. I accept the miraculous task of leading me forward.
- I bring soothing inner and outer calm. I represent respectful stability, safety, consensus, integrity. I water my garden, pull up the weeds, plant and tend the seeds.
- I trust myself. I show up. I don't give up. I won't leave.
- I am the Sovereign archetype of **healing** and **wholeness**.

> *"I think midlife is when the universe gently places her hands on your shoulders,*
> *Pulls you close, and whispers in your ear;*
> *Its time. All of this pretending and performing –*
> *These coping mechanisms, that you've developed to protect yourself*
> *From feeling inadequate and getting hurt – it has to go.*
> *Your armour is preventing you from growing into your gifts.*
> *I understand that you needed these protections*
> *When you were small.*
> *I understand that you believed your armour*
> *Could help you secure all of the things you needed*
> *To feel worthy of love and belonging,*
> *Time is growing short.*
> *There are unexplored adventures ahead of you.*
> *It is time for you to show up and be seen."*
>
> *Brene Brown*

- Coming to consciousness is a long, painful struggle and requires great courage. I choose to release my ego-building Hero's journey by integrating my striving Warrior into my characterful, soulful mid-life. I regulate my work and activity in the world so I can slow down and take time to get to know myself. I create space and situations where I build my Kingship so I can refine myself to maturity.
- I create a foundational **home** within my heart. I express my individuality and dare to be all of myself.
- I include everyone I love in my evolution. Everyone I love is here. We shelter and encourage each other.
- Accepting that only I can rescue myself from myself, I am guided and prompted by my **Soul** to re-examine all of my life, the fundamental kaleidoscope of my character.
- I am not trying to fix, cure, or even make healthy. I don't want perfection, safety or a trouble-free life. I want to be close to myself, close to life. I don't want to save myself. I want to know and accept myself, my beautiful and my painful, all of me.
- As a generative life force, I hold my middle ground while I collect and re-possess myself. I accept everything I find within, all my shadowy, frightening and strange, lonely and sorrowful, masculine and feminine. I slowly make them conscious, so my opposing forces unite and empower unifying abundance.
- The first step is to **know myself.**
- This first step, my experience of self-discovery, is the most important. Just by seeing and acknowledging the truth of myself. I shine my light on myself and see who is there.

> "I hold a beast, an angel, and a madman in me,
> And my enquiry is as to their working,
> and my problem is their subjugation and victory,
> down throw and upheaval,
> and my effort is their self-expression."
> Dylan Thomas

- I am attentive to myself so that, once I know myself, I bring **creative healing by reorganising my character**.
- I bring legitimate order, inclusive unity, and healing grace to nurture who I am. I change the world by healing myself. I bring compassion to my welcoming search. I ask myself, "what ails thee"?
- I create my world of harmony, evolving self-knowledge, authenticity, and kind-hearted connection.
- I hold the vision of the beauty and goodness of life and guide all towards profound love.
- I bring all to my refined Kingly heart, welcoming all parts of myself into the transmuting depth of my being. As I rebirth myself, I am reborn. I add beauty, acceptance and love, growing myself more fully alive, recognising my life in its astonishing magnificence. Incorporating my shadow, I address the parts of myself that push me, the Sovereign, off my throne so I am no longer present.
- Accepting that I am always in the process of becoming, I rediscover and adjust the mosaic of my character, miraculously returning to the poetry of who I have always been.
- I **bring peace to myself.**
- Knowing that only I can bring peace to myself, I choose to make inner peace. I accept myself completely. I make a home of acceptance and love.
- I create a sacred marriage between my King and all my many parts. I marry all parts of myself by knowing them and lovingly drawing them into the home of my heart, where I give them a place to belong and respectfully create a lifetime relationship with them.
- I gentle my sharp edges; I strengthen where I break easily. I love my lost, afraid and ugly. I find the gold in my sad, muddy wasteland. I am kind to myself; I love the parts of myself I was ashamed of and hated. I heal myself. I let my suffering crack me into humility and compassion. I bless my battered heart to flower.
- I accept that everything I need is within me.
- I create a world of love by **firstly loving myself.**

> "The return to love is hardly the end of life's adventure.
> It's the real beginning.
> Denying love is the only problem and embracing it is the only answer."
> Marianne Williamson

- When I look deep into my own heart, I see that I was born for love. Knowing this, I awaken and blossom into love. I drink love in. I surrender to love. When asked to name all the things I love, I name myself first.
- I know that the love I build in my heart is my true inheritance, that it is true and strong and that the gold in my love blesses all it touches.
- I accept that I deserve my beautiful, gentle love, and kind affection, along with everyone else.
- I acknowledge that the degree to which I don't love myself is the degree to which I cannot let love in.
- My love, stewarded by my King, initiates the second half of my life.
- As the regenerative Golden Sovereign, I exercise the **power of love**. I renounce my desire for power over others and my lust for power for myself. I do not resign myself to no power. I welcome the freedom and privilege of power with.
- My love transforms. My love heals, wins over all pain and misfortune, and brings back to life. It is wise and sees all. The beauty of my love changes the world. Love is eternal, and with the power of my love, anything is possible.
- I **love**. Love is the ground of my being.
- The circle of my love is strong, positive and beautiful. From its centre to its circumference, my love is the glue that binds my Kingdom together; it's life-giving water.
- As the wholehearted, great-hearted King, I live from my heart. My heart is my compass. I know and trust my love.
- Love pulls all of life together. It builds a bridge between me and everything. It is life's greatest gift. I unfold into love, and it opens my senses. Love is my juice, and without it, I dry up.
- **Joy** is the dynamic currency of my Kingship. It is in me, not in things or my circumstances.
- Joy flows from me because I have come to know, love, settle and include all the parts of myself that previously blocked my joy.
- From the Divine, I formulate, hold and make real my **King's Calling.**
- I know why I am here. I hold the vision and the mission of my Kingdom. I ensure that all in my world is tuned to serve my Guiding Light.
- My King's first mission and vision are for my family. I am the father King at home before any other effort in the world. My family is the ground I live on that gives me life. I learn and model my Kingship in my own home first.
- My King's Calling is the highest expression of my love for the world. It sings the song of my heart and holds my greatest gifts which make a difference to the lives of others. Living my Calling brings me refined energy and sublime success, and delivering it, I achieve the vital, expressive, prosperous life I wish for.
- I am responsible for discovering and building my **Gifts** so I can contribute them to the world.
- It is my responsibility to recognize, cultivate, awaken and bless by genius gifts. Once I have bought my gifts alive, my ambitious aspiration is to live and contribute them as my loving service to the world. It doesn't matter if my gifts are small or huge; it just matters that I bring them alive and deliver them with all my heart.

> *"Let us all do what is right,*
> *Strive with all our might towards the unattainable,*
> *Develop as fully as we can the gifts God has given us,*
> *And never stop learning."*
> Ludwig van Beethoven

- I offer **my genius to the world.**
- The spirit of genius is already in me. It wants to be uncovered and practised into manifestation for the good of all. I look within to discover it; I search myself to find and unfold it without limitation into the world.

> *"Neither a lofty degree of intelligence nor imagination*
> *Nor both together go into the making of a genius.*
> *Love, love, love, that is the soul of genius."*
> Wolfgang Amadeus Mozart

- **I am authentic. I know my intrinsic value**, and I appreciate yours. I am grateful for and accept myself, and I hope you do the same for yourself.
- My authenticity starts in my heart and expresses itself as joy of being myself. I know life intimately, and I respect myself for getting through.
- I have faith in myself. I am comfortable being me because I know and accept who I am. Authenticity is my highest form and expression. I am honest and transparent.
- **I believe in myself.** I develop myself to be the best I can be. I enhance and evolve my brilliant gifts and bestow my talents on the world. I enrich the world for the better.
- I hold myself together, whether I am succeeding or failing.
- Following my Kings Guiding Vision, I create **success and abundance**.
- I create independence, wealth, security, service and prestige.
- I am the source of fertility for the realm. I am nature, and when I flourish, rain falls, the sun shines, the crops grow. I am generative and generous. I am grateful for abundance; I believe in it, and promote it. I dream it into existence.
- I am **ambitious** and always looking to see how I can advance myself and those around me. I use my success to create a better world.
- I accept the challenge I set myself to make a significant contribution. I do not shy away. I am steadfast in my dedication and efforts.
- I am **sacred**. I relax into my Soul and open myself to its nudges and prompts. As the link between the human world and the Divine world, I manifest the sacred order of the Universe. I am the channel from the eternal world, the central artery that brings Divine love into the human world.

- I acknowledge that the Sovereign archetype holds great power. I know that when I truly step into my Kingship my life will change in ways I have never experienced before. I accept that I need to be ready for this, and when it happens, I must make sure I keep a close eye on my Tyrant King.
- I embody the generative union of **masculine and feminine**. This union expresses my libido, my generative and inclusive fertile life force.
- I am married to my Kingdom, my partner, and the earth. Our creative, regenerative partnership brings a harvest of bounty and abundance into our world.
- I love the feminine. I have made peace with the feminine, and am reclaiming the feminine aspects of myself I lost long ago. I love the joyful flowering this brings me.

Sovereign Responsibilities and Capabilities

Everything I dream of is possible, but it is up to me to create it. The only part of me that can do this beautifully is my Sovereign.
The following are the core responsibilities of the King, the areas of his life to which he can bring his inspiring capabilities.

- **I manage change.**
- I accept that wholeness includes both creation and destruction. I respond to my desire to evolve and I release beliefs that hold me back. I know that when I make space inside with an ending, I create opportunities for the next creative step of my journey.
- I exercise the power of **choice**. I know myself, and I know what I am choosing. I pronounce my decision. The more choice I have, the more expansive is my Sovereignty.
- My choices create my future. My decisions create my life. I am responsible for the results I get. That is my joy. My choices give me the power of creation.
- I evolve past the life I was born into. I choose the path I create. I know that when I make a powerful choice for the good of all, the universe gets behind me and supports my courage.
- **I create peace.**
- I slowly change my old opinions, search within for all the parts of me that are not at peace, and build a new inner world based on love and inclusion. I reclaim peace for myself, and I reflect it outwards to the world.
- As the Sovereign, I am the **servant leader**. I serve my King's Calling, my vision for the world. I follow this star, my gifted service. I lead from my heart, supported by my head.
- I build community. I build trust within relationships and help others come together. I do not compete but build consensus. I drive out fear. I eliminate the fake and the false. I remain humble. I encourage myself and all present to be genuinely ourselves, to build and manifest our sovereignty.

- I create a life of **service**.
- I optimistically dream of a better world, and I endeavour to bring this idealistic world into being. Through service, I offer something to the world that will outlast me. I leave behind a legacy that nourishes the world.
- Service offers a path to greatness. With my heart full of grace and my soul with love, I build a life where service is my bread and butter, my fire and oxygen. Offering love in action, I serve the world.
- As the King, I rule my **speech**, my self-expression, which lets the outer world know what is in me. I do not speak negatively, and I do not lie. My word is my bond.
- My words are powerful. With my voice I pronounce my decisions, I express love, I bless and support.
- I **listen** to witness and empathise with your truth. I bless and validate you by giving you my full attention. For me, you are an undiscovered world, and I relish getting to know you.
- **I Model the Father Archetype**

> "The heart of a father is the masterpiece of nature."
> Prevost Abbe

- I embody the archetype of the Father God in masculine form. I have regal depth. I am the archetype of the **good** encouraging **father**, of nurturing fatherhood. I warmly channel the light of the sun. I treasure the earth and cherish the feminine, my children, and my home. I model the loving protective father who cherishes, holds and encourages his children.
- I **mentor**.

> "We're all just walking each other home."
> Ram Dass

- As a role model who inspires, I motivate you to achieve greatness. I become a mirror for you to see yourself in. I nurture and build, seeking to understand and magnify the best in you.
- I call forth your true potential and create a fertile field for you to blossom. I encourage you with patience, and I am always there for you when you need me. I give you space to dance your unique self to life.

Sovereign Gifts and Expressions of the Power of his Love

Your Sovereign has particular gifts that are your inheritance, and which magnify and pronounce your love for the world. It is your privilege to manifest your gifts abundantly.

- I am **present, awake, and aware**. To stay present, I have made terms with my mind.
- I stand back from my thoughts and witness them. I don't automatically go along with them. I observe my thoughts, but I don't join them and react. I don't allow my thoughts to do things to me or frighten me.
- I **create light**.
- I attract light from its hidden source in the Universe, where it shines on all things, and I release it into the world. My Sovereign energy burns brightly, shines like the sunrise, and brings light into the world.
- I am the archetype of **blessing**.
- I give blessing. I heal with my blessing. My blessings have psychological and spiritual power. When I bless, I enhance and amplify.
- I am inspired and **enthusiastic**. I have abundant **energy, passion and drive**. I am excited about what I do. My enthusiasm inspires others, and I sweep them along with me with appreciation and encouragement.
- I love my Kingdom as a realm of heartfelt **generosity**.
- I am naturally compassionate. Life, love and generosity flow from me.
- With generosity, I create the future by giving all to life right now.
- To those around me, I give of myself. I offer encouragement, support and a sympathetic heart.
- I am **grateful**. I give thanks for my good fortune.
- I create good fortune by giving first. I send a magnificent wave of loving service out into the world and rejoice as its karmic echo floods back across my life. Gratitude is magnetic, and the more I feel, the more light and abundance I attract into my life.
- **Beauty**

"The voice of beauty speaks softly; it creeps only into the most fully awakened souls."
Friedrich Nietzsche

- Like many of these qualities that are the King's inheritance, beauty shines. It seems luminous, summoning, drawing towards itself, mesmerizing. The King is a beauty gold mine. The King's nature is to create, radiate, appreciate, and be a gateway into beauty.
- **Hope and Faith**
- I notice how my heart rises with hope in a pronounced upsurge of excitement, love and trust. Hope brightens my heart and future. She promises peace and tells me everything will be alright, that I can trust that life will be as I hoped and trusted it could be; beautiful for all of us.

- Hope is optimistic. Faith believes in the best. They make a stand for good.
- I am **humble and compassionate.**
- I am equal to all men. I am not superior to anyone. I concentrate on making sure I am superior to my former self rather than other people. I don't compare myself with others.
- **Wonder**

> *"Wonder is the beginning of wisdom."*
> Socrates

- When I feel wonder, it's not about me. It is a feeling that comes from what is running through me. Wonder is love, joy, and celebration entwined
- **I deliberately create my legacy.**

> *"The things you do for yourself are gone when you are gone,*
> *but the things you do for others remain as your legacy."*
> Kalu Ndukwe Kalu

- I do not leave creating a legacy to the end of my life. I attend to creating a legacy as a way of living my life. My life's effort is to serve and benefit the world with my work while I live and strive and profoundly inspire and benefit future generations.

The Heart King Speaks

Each paragraph is the voice of a different man in his Heart King.

"I do this for a sense of purpose, for responsibility, to be seen, to set an example of how to do things right, to be appreciated and acknowledged."

"I hold the space where my true self can be. I bring out the authentic and genuine, by including both the crumbling and tyrant kings. I am the golden thread between these two. I listen to each to bring in the fuller picture. I bring tenacity and commitment to the greater good, and a strong desire for peace."

"My heart is a flower bee's come to. I absolutely love everyone. I do nothing except this, so healing and transformation naturally unfold. I am deeply connected to my ancestors, Jesus, deep spirituality, and the love that pervades everything. I look at people and see myself. I feel total peace. Nothing needs to be done. The stories around what needs to be done seem funny, like children's games. Fear tries to pull me out of being into doing, from complete trust into fear that I have to do something to make it ok."

"I am ok just as I am. I completely trust my abilities. I create a safe loving space for deep healing by following my instinct, moment by moment, with no agenda."

"I have a big, kind, generous heart. It's been wounded enough times in enough ways for me to hold people in hurt. I am the ground I need so I don't merge or collude, but just witness and hold space."

"I can be fierce and tender. I trust my wisdom. I trust what wisdom comes through me. I say, and I do the right thing. People feel safe to be with me. I am safe to be with, because I know my shadows. I know the dangerous and dark places within myself. My grief is deep and beautiful. I have a fierce commitment to protecting my heart because it is needed."

"I want to be in the river of my feelings, where I can connect with mine, and with the kingdom."

"I bring deep connection to the brilliance of all my parts. I bring connection to my predator, my lineage, my ancestors. I bring deep searing potential to who I can be."

"I know and integrate all of myself. I know what it means to be awake and aware. The Magician is awake to awareness. I am awake to my heart, to unity of being. I bring all into my unified vision. I am awake to the ground of my being."

"I am living from depth. I see through my heart. I feel into what I am looking at. My heart is my perceptual centre. My heart is awake. My spiritual heart is open and available to whatever is happening. My heart is my ground, my centre of being."

"I am centred, no matter what is going on around or inside me. I have a presence that is eternal and unchanging, connected into the nature of all existence. Here is stand, both individual and the whole of it."

"I love myself whole-heartedly. Not only my magnificent nature but the grim, dark, hidden and destructive parts, my animal nature and my coldness. I am not the source of all light but the balance point between light and dark, the focal point where true transformation happens with the slightest of effort. I know where to make that effort for healing and change."

"I know my gifts are needed in this world, I know I have brilliance to bring. I hunt for those areas of myself that stop me doing this or being what I need to be. I have a strong focus of attention that allows me to do this, a deep compassion that keeps me focussed and an openness to what my gifts could be. I love the exploration."

The Sovereign's Journey of self-knowledge and mature evolution

You have looked at the archetype of the Healthy King. You have seen how you behave as your King, with your admirable capabilities and joyful life-giving gifts.

You have listed the qualities of your King you are familiar with and recognize in yourself.

You have also started to get some idea of what is still to be developed in your Kingship. Now you have some awareness of the areas you can focus on and cultivate to deepen your Sovereignty.

Being in Right Relation with the King Archetype

As you step into the archetype of your King, you are stepping into an ancient, powerful nourishing regal force of love, healing, integration and evolution.

Any time you embrace an archetype, you step into its force-field. The King archetype bestows energy and power. When you build your King, it doesn't mean that you become the 'King of the World'. It means you are a man who steps into the dominion of the King archetype and seeks to harness and express it in himself. If you believe you are the 'King of the World', it means you are in Too Much King. It is important to remember this because it is easy to inflate with this potent dynamism when you step into your Kingship.

As you get used to being in your King's authority, you will need to pay attention to stay in the right relationship with this powerful archetypal force. For me, it was a sharp learning to reside in and express the power of my Heart King without becoming an inflated, grandiose Tyrant.

One practice that helps is to keep a correct reasonable distance from this powerful archetype. I keep a healthy distance from the King's force. If I don't, I start to believe I am the great, all-powerful King, and I tend towards grandiosity and narcissism. If you imagine the earth circling the sun in its proper orbit, you can consider the earth as yourself, and the sun as your Golden King energy. If your earthly self keeps its correct orbit around the sun, all is well. If, however, your earth slips its established orbit and comes closer to the sun, it overheats. Or, if it drifts off course and slips away from the sun, it freezes over.

The King, or the sun, is life-giving, so the right relationship with this life source depends on engaging with it in a slightly detached, non-identified way and keeping the correct established distance from it.

As you become the Golden Heart King, you will gradually become infused with powerful archetypal King energy. This force will become available to you so that you can, as the King, channel it to benefit all within your Kingdom. You will become suffused with the archetype and will be able to create for yourself and the world in a way that is not possible without it. You then hold the King's responsibility to steward this energy for the good of all. You will face the temptation to slip into Tyrant King and take all the good for yourself.

You may be tempted to refuse the call of your higher self and shy away from becoming the Heart King. If you shy away from this powerful force, you run the risk of drifting out of orbit into the passive shadow of the King, detached, abdicating and distant. If you don't become the true King when it is your time, you deprive yourself and the world of this powerful force.

Starving yourself of King energy is not a neutral position. It will result in your behaving as the Abdicator. You will be in danger of drying up, being coldly out of touch with this igniting, warming, infusing, sunny energy. Abdicating your greatness, you may become feeble, ineffective and helpless. If you refuse to take up your King, you turn this force over to others. You release some of the power of your life to them.

It is a delicate balance to live as your true Heart King. As you bring the power of the King archetype into your world, all three Kings are empowered. To stay on the road of your Heart King without falling into your Abdicator or inflating into your Tyrant is the elegant, challenging path of true Kingship.

The Sovereign's Journey into his Underworld

Now that you have a sense and feel of your Sovereign, you have unearthed your higher self. As your Sovereign you can conduct yourself and your life as a beautiful act of love. This is the Sovereign we all seek to embed within, yet this is not an instantaneous happening. Our Sovereign does not just appear because we appreciate our Sovereign qualities. To build a King who is good enough, a King who loves and is strong, a King who creates and holds his creation in service of the world, requires love, ability, and strength. As we progress along our Sovereign's Journey we face many of the challenges Kings have faced since the beginning of time.

The main challenge we face on our journey is ourself. Embarking on our Sovereign's Journey, our first effort will be to get to know ourself inside out. Our inner world is made up of many different characters and parts, all with their own essence, ways of being, wants, desires and feelings. Your next step will be to get to know all these different parts of yourself, all these different expressions of your being.

Our Human Journey is pretty tough for most of us, and often especially hard when we were children and teenagers. All of us have been wounded by an unkind world and by unkind people. Sadly, for us all, this wounding affects who we are. It hurts, and we develop ways of being aimed at not having the same hurt happen again. Our wounded Golden Boy and Golden Teenager reacts and either fights against, and becomes the Too Much King as an adult, and acts as a bit of a Tyrant King. Or he gives in, and accepts he is powerless, and grows into the Crumbling King.

These are the two brother Kings we have alongside our Heart Sovereign. Both wounded, one aggressive and dominating, the other weak and abdicating.

Neither of these two Kings are supposedly socially acceptable. It seems to me though that traditional Patriarchal society is mostly based on the Tyrant archetype. Our world rewards Tyrants who are forceful and ruthless enough to get their own way. As for the Crumbling King, we hardly see him as he is struggling, unhappy and unable to create the world his heart desires.

In the next part of your Sovereign Journey you will get to know your Abdicating King and your Tyrant King.

While previously we have been inhabiting the best of ourselves in our Heart Sovereign, we are now diving down into parts of ourselves where we are not our best. We are now taking the Sovereign underworld journey to individuation and the integration of opposites. We are entering the land of pain and dysfunction, of lost love, betrayal, abuse, hurt and suffering; a version of our own personal underground hell.

In life we have developed ways of behaving to avoid, evade, forget, and run away from our pain, and these behaviours form the basis of our Crumbling and Tyrant Kings.

We try to hide these wounded dysfunctional parts of ourselves, from others and from ourselves. However, hidden or not, all internal characters get their chance to live out at some time. When we are exhausted or hurt our harder, impatient, controlling Tyrant King comes out, or we collapse and Abdicate. We can't stop it. The same applies to all the many different wounded parts of us.

It takes a lot of energy and strength to resist and not become the domineering Tyrant. It is not easy to hold ourself out of our Crumbling King's depressed, apathetic orbit.

It is a constant struggle not to become these two Kings.

It's Time for a Different Approach

At this stage of your Sovereign's Journey you are going to do the opposite of what you have always done. Instead of trying to hide your Tyrant King and your Crumbling King, you are going to turn towards them so you can get to know your brother Kings and bring them to the light of your consciousness. You are doing this to know yourself and to bring your Sovereign into close relationship with these parts of you so you can work with them and regulate their effect on your world.

You are heading into your underworld, your unconscious, so it is good to have an idea of where you are going so you can dive in deeply and also keep yourself safe. This is where your trauma resides, and your reaction to it. Held out of sight your original hurts live on in the parts of you who suffered traumatic wounding. How much the trauma you endured will have affected you depends on many factors, including the degree of love and care your received and the severity and duration of the wounding events. The coping strategies you used to keep going in the face of the trauma became your habits, and in time became unconscious. The younger parts of you that experienced the wounding still inhabit this underworld and long for healing.

Because these parts are still active and alive inside us they affect our world. If something happens that resembles our earlier wounding then all our younger traumatised parts kick off and behave as if their original wounding is happening again. We feel our original pain and react in our usual ways. We feel our trauma again.

On our retreats we facilitate the King to hold and love this trauma and our wounded younger parts. We can't do that here. The best way for you to keep as safe as possible here is to build your Heart King as your base, and to learn a bit about trauma and how your trauma affects you. If you wish to do this have a look at resources in Appendix 1.

Your two wounded Kings are complicated characters, with many different facets and behaviours. Not all they demonstrate will apply to you, and as the Tyrant and the Crumbling Kings you will have your own particular ways of being not shown here. Your aim is to unearth these characters in yourself.

You can start with your Crumbling King.

The Crumbling King Archetype

It is time to get to know your King who struggles, who believes you are 'not good enough'. This is your King who does not believe in you, who believes you can't do it. Your Crumbling King cannot create the world your heart knows is possible.

And what he believes is true. Sad though it is, this is the part of us that holds and experiences our failures, our stumbles and falls. Our Struggling King tries but he messes up. He is full of shame and is relentlessly attacked by our Self-critic for being not good enough.

While the Tyrant is more visible and alive in our world, my experience is that far more men suffer by living their Crumbling King. I find that the belief of being "not good enough" is an epidemic amongst men. If this is your strongest King you will suffer and struggle in life.

Consciously inhabiting our Crumbling King is such a relief. When we deliberately give this part of us space to show himself our Heart Sovereign can start to get into relationship with a part of ourselves that we would normally shun or hide. While it is difficult and painful to get to know our Crumbling King it is also a relief to pull this part of ourselves out of his unkempt, ignored dungeon and into the light of our Heart King.

When we are stuck in our Crumbling King and he is firmly collapsed onto our throne his hold is strong and sadly familiar so that he feels he is our whole world. However, when we bring him to light we realise that he is only one part of us, and that our Heart King is evolving us so that we don't have to be stuck in our Crumbling King. Bringing him to awareness will drastically weaken his hold on us. This is true for all the archetypal parts of you that your Heart King brings to the light of your awareness.

We will start by looking at how a boy is injured, which results in him living the wounded rather than the healthy aspect of the Sovereign archetype.

How a Boy is Wounded

Every boy has particular essential core needs in his childhood. These include a requirement for stability, steadfast love, acceptance, consistent and affirmative holding, attention and approval. Every boy needs to be loved for who he is. As he grows, he takes in the best qualities he sees in both his parents and builds them into himself. When his parents encourage and validate these qualities and bless the boy's unique character, he slowly forms his self-image and sense of self.

If the beautiful Golden Boy finds out that he is not loved and blessed for being himself, he learns from his parents or caregivers that there is something wrong with how he naturally is or how he usually expresses himself. He understands that being himself gets him in trouble. This breaks his early development so that he cannot construct a sense of self that is solid and realistic. He has no foundation of self and has to rely on others for the attention that will help him feel accepted and alive.

These experiences lead him to believe that he is flawed in some way. His self-absorbed parents tell him he is too much or too "big for his boots". Alternatively, they may be suffocatingly overinvolved, so they try to live through him, giving him no room to establish his sense of self. Maybe he makes mistakes and is criticised for being "not good enough". The boy then tries to change himself to be whoever he hopes is "good enough". He learns that he can't be himself. To be accepted and loved, he has to be someone else. This realisation creates a great wound inside him. It is a heart-breaking betrayal of his unique essence and his sense of himself.

When our boy believes he is not good enough, he also receives the message that he is not important. He takes this to mean that he is not worthy of love. All further damaging actions and words inflicted on him for the rest of his childhood add to and strengthen his belief. He carries this image of himself into adulthood.

Below are some ways a boy ends up believing he is "not good enough".

Family Behaviour that Wound a Boy's sense of self:
- Rejection. Telling a boy that he is unwanted, that he is worthless, that he should have been the opposite sex, that he is not your offspring.
- Constantly criticising, verbally humiliating, publicly ridiculing, and putting him down in front of his peers.
- Withholding love and approval, denigrating joy and pleasure, excluding him from family or social events.
- Neglecting, physically abandoning, threatening abandonment, telling him he was adopted or didn't belong to the family, threatening to throw him out of the family home.
- Unpredictable love and attention.
- Providing a lack of direction, supervision, limits or guidance.
- Expecting the boy to look after his parents, making him care for his younger siblings, blaming him for his sibling's behaviour, getting him to run the home, and wanting him to provide financial support.
- Not modelling taking responsibility, and not letting the child make any decisions.

Resulting Beliefs
- In the face of this relentless damage to his Sovereign essence, the boy either gives up and accepts damaging beliefs about himself, or he fights against these beliefs and tries too hard to prove he is not what he has been labelled.
- In reality, he probably swings in a bipolar fashion between believing these beliefs and fighting against them.

Giving in to his Beliefs
- I am not good enough. I can't be myself. I am not worthy. I'm worthless. I have no value. I am nobody.
- Other people are uncaring and unreliable. No one is interested in nurturing me. I cannot rely on anyone for support, protection or strength.
- I will be abandoned because people are unstable, unpredictable, and erratic. They will suddenly disappear. They will leave me for someone better.
- I am inferior. I compare myself and come out less than you. I am inadequate, a lower status to others.
- I am self-conscious and insecure. You will blame me, criticise and reject me.

- I have no direction. I will never be successful. I will always be a failure. I can't make the right decisions.
- I am helpless. I need you to help me. I cannot do it on my own.
- I avoid all responsibility. I can't commit. I have no integrity.
- I am desperate for your attention, approval and recognition. I give up myself to fit in. My self-esteem depends on your reactions to me.
- I cannot be joyful or happy.

In adulthood, this wounded King now lives out his beliefs about himself that he developed in childhood. He believes in the belittling, abusive, neglectful, bullying lessons he learned and all their shaming messages. The power of his ingrained inner beliefs expresses themselves in his life through his actions which bring his wounded Shadow King's to the fore.

Believing this about himself as a child, he grows into the Crumbling King, who suffers from the same wounds as the Tyrant but expresses them differently. Rather than fighting against his beliefs, he gives in to them.

Read through the behaviours of this Crumbling King archetype and notice which you recognise in yourself. Take time with your perusal. Tap into the energetic field of this archetype. Feel into him for yourself. As you identify aspects of yourself in the outline you are reading, notice how your Crumbling King plays out in your life.

What other ways does this struggling King show up in your thoughts and actions? This list of behaviours is here for you as a starting point, so you can recognise how the Crumbling King archetype behaves. In what other ways, not listed here, do you act as this King? Note them down to start building a picture of your Crumbling King.

Wounded Behaviour of the Crumbling King Archetype

- I pursue the path of abdication, of **no power**. I am powerless. I hide my gifts. I don't trust myself.
- I'm not good enough. I'm afraid that I'm worthless. I believe that I don't have value. I don't value myself. I feel passive, dependent, inadequate, and inferior.
- I have **low self-esteem**. I'm not good enough as me. I am full of self-doubt. I have no self-confidence. I am inadequate and unacceptable.
- When I look inside, I don't know who's there. I am afraid to look for lost pieces of myself. I am all fragmented, in bits. I can't put myself together. I have disowned parts of myself that no longer trust me.

"That is the way it is with a wound.
The wound begins to close in on itself, to protect what is hurting so much.
And once it is closed, you no longer see what is underneath, what started the pain."
Amy Tan

- I don't love myself. I have a hole in my heart. I hate myself. I can't relax, nurture myself or enjoy life.
- I am depressed, despairing, stagnated, old too early, and over the hill. I am paralysed, fearful and indecisive.
- I deny my skills, inhibit my growth and disparage my accomplishments. I obliterate myself. I do not accept compliments.

> "Don't you see? The catastrophe is me.
> My very existence is an affront to everything that is natural and good."
> K.J. Wignall

- I **abdicate** myself and **abandon** my world. I am not prepared to hold my inner realm or love, accept and integrate all parts of myself. I have no centre.
- I don't trust leaders, and I don't trust my leadership.
- My abdication and inability to live according to my Sovereign's Guiding Light has disastrous consequences for my Kingdom. The land dies, the sun's rays weaken, winter grips the land, the rains fail, the rivers dry up, and the crops will not grow.
- Like a bad habit, even though I am the Abdicator, I am difficult to dislodge when I am on the throne. I am comfortable, old familiar pain. I collapse, and my depression holds me in an awful, tight grip. I suffocate and suck the life out of my other more positive, healthy parts, and my despairing inertia keeps me in place.
- My lack of strength and centre means I cannot protect my Kingdom, so confusion, chaos, and destruction rule. Enemies arise to challenge me, and pain and violence annihilate goodness and hope.
- I have abandoned justice. No one and no part is safe. Evil, rebellion, and misconduct thrive.
- I do not hold my family. I am immature and timid. I am impotent. I am not present when I am around. I am absent. My family suffers without me, and pain, loss, resentment and disorder manifest.
- I am a disappointment to others. I have let them down. I feel empty, and I do not measure up.
- I give up what is important to me to follow what I think is important to you. I abandon my heart's longing and give up my core vision to follow yours. I no longer know what I want. I am not authentic. My niceness, smiling, and submissive behaviour is my defence mechanism. I abandon my own ambitions to make others look good.

> "Self-abandoned, relaxed and effortless, I seemed to have laid me down in the dried-up bed of a great river; I heard a flood loosened in remote mountains, I felt the torrent come; to rise I had no will, to flee I had no strength."
> Charlotte Brontë

- I abandon my needs for yours. When I try to meet my needs, I worry that I am demanding, selfish and needy. I have no real value on my own, but only in relation to you. I live your life rather than mine. You complete me as I am not enough on my own.

- I have no rights. It is not right for me to pursue what I want for myself. I am here to serve others. I put others first. I sacrifice myself for you. Sacrificing myself gives me some sense of self-worth. I keep myself in a position of weakness. If I do try to assert myself, I feel frightened and guilty and worry that I will hurt or diminish you or that you will attack me. I have no right to get out of this situation.
- I end up exhausted because I do not get my needs met. Internally I am profoundly lacking.
- **I won't take responsibility.** I need you to take responsibility for areas of my life.
- I agree to do things I believe are wrong, so I don't lose your support.
- I won't take the initiative or initiate projects because I have no confidence in my judgments or abilities.
- I neglect the ordinary world and ignore even my most pressing problems. I bury my head in distractions and don't deal with real life.
- I don't know how to go forward. I am unsure about my next steps. I don't know where I am going. I fear going forward, so stay stuck or even retreat. I can't create new choices.
- I sell out. I betray myself for an easy life. I take the softest option.
- I blame you for my problems.
- I excuse myself. I am too old. My unsuccessful career is not my fault. I was not responsible for all my broken relationships. It was their fault. It is because the world is against me that none of my noble ideas came to reality.

> "The moment we begin to fear the opinions of others and hesitate to tell the truth that is in us, and from motives of policy are silent when we should speak, the divine floods of light and life no longer flow into our souls."
> Elizabeth Cady Stanton

- I am a **failure**. Everything I try to do goes wrong. Because of this, I won't commit to anything.
- If it looks like I am going to be successful, I sabotage, procrastinate, blame, and don't complete. I suddenly leave my job, change careers or get ill.
- I am not wanted. People don't like me. I carry the failure, the disappointment, and all the shit that no one else wants. I feel blamed, excluded, shunned, and avoided.
- No one respects me. I am ignored. I am not relevant. I am forgotten.
- I can't speak up. I can't put myself forward. I can't make my views known. I believe no one will listen to me or take me seriously.
- I am not good enough. I am not worthy
- It's not safe. It's not safe for me to be myself. It's not safe for me to be successful.
- It's too difficult for me to **make decisions**. I become anxious when I have to decide. I need excessive advice and reassurance. I need you to make up my mind for me.

- I can't guide myself. I cannot connect to my inner guidance. I am all over the place, swinging between different influences, staying with the strongest until a new authority appears.
- I don't want to make decisions that could result in me taking risks, making mistakes, or being in conflict or trouble.

> *"Hold fast to dreams,*
> *For if dreams die*
> *Life is a broken-winged bird,*
> *That cannot fly."*
> *Langston Hughes*

- **I am weak.** I am passive and inferior to you, so I go to great lengths to get you to nurture and **support me**. I can't fend for myself. If you don't look after me, I will quickly find someone else who will. If you don't help, I will fall apart and maybe kill myself.
- I feel **helpless** and uncomfortable when alone and seize up with strangled fear. Please help me. You are much more capable than me.
- I only exist to please you. If I try to assert or please myself, I fear you will reject and abandon me.
- I can't move forward without you backing me up. I need you to be my mentor and regulate me. I don't trust myself, so I need to find someone I can trust.
- I need you to approve of me, and I feel scolded when you don't. I will be submissive and dependent on you, so you want to take care of me. I cling to you and can't live without your help. I seek overprotection and dominance from you.
- I see myself as helpful to you, but in reality, I'm a burden, a heavy weight for you. My efforts to manipulate you into caring for me are tiring for you.
- I am over-loyal to friends and family, but only because I am afraid of being abandoned and left without support.
- I am **afraid to speak out,** to speak my truth. I freeze and hold my breath to lock up my throat. I choke up.
- I can't voice what I want to say. What I don't say gets stuck in my body.
- I am ashamed to bring my inside out, so I hide my essence and block my true feelings and expression.
- I cannot initiate challenging conversations, ask difficult questions, or hold others to account.

> *"I'm just one long disappointment.*
> *But I live, I live, with an absolutely continuous sense of failure. I am always defeated, always."*
> *Iris Murdoch*

- I am **shy**. I won't step into the light. I don't want attention, and I don't wish for status.
- I don't want you to make demands on me. If you do, I don't say no but comply in a passive-aggressive way.
- I am evasive and indecisive. I give mixed signals and seem unpredictable.

- I present myself as entirely harmless, even though sooner or later, I stick a knife in your back.
- My depression sucks out my life force and withers my success, prosperity, and courage. I am **depressed**. I am down, sad, hopeless, numb and apathetic.
- I don't have enough energy. I'm tired but can't sleep properly. I wake up early and then struggle to get out of bed. I'm exhausted.
- I am dissatisfied. I'm empty and sterile. I'm worthless. I'm ashamed of myself. It's my fault.
- My fear and sadness dominate me. I try not to feel. It hurts so much. It's easier to have no emotions.
- I am pessimistic. There's no point. The world has betrayed me. It's all going to go wrong anyway.
- I'm shit. I want to kill myself. I want to get away from all this.

> "Sometimes I can hear my bones straining under the weight of all the lives I'm not living."
> Jonathan Safran Foer

- I allay with the wounded parts of my magician, warrior, and lover. I listen to and **believe my critical, judging internal predatorial voices**. I belittle my abilities and put myself down. I am paranoid and impotent. Everywhere I look, I see people conspiring against me.
- Your criticism and disapproval confirm that I am useless and worthless. I quickly lose faith in myself.
- I am hiding because I fear my flaws will be exposed. I keep hidden and isolated. I make sure that I am not heard, and then I feel ignored.
- I have secrets. I hide. I am corrupt. I take bribes, cheat and lie.
- I won't be true to myself. I am deceived, cheated and lied to by others.
- I am **over-focused on security**.
- When will I have enough to know I am truly secure? I hang on to items I no longer need. I won't spend money on myself.
- I try to keep safe by staying small.
- I get anxious when you separate from me.
- When I'm in your life, I **act generous and unselfish**, but underneath I want **something back from you**. I have high expectations of what you will give me in return and resent and cast you aside when I don't get it.
- I do not acknowledge my emotional needs and try to get them met in unconscious and underhand ways, such as by sacrificing myself for you. I try to get the love I want by always putting you first. Having put you first, I am secretly angry and resentful of you.
- I **idealise you** and see great qualities in you that I can't see in myself. I need your approval and validation. I fear your displeasure and the loss of your love. I can't separate from you or rebel against you.

- I cannot bless you or myself. Even so, I thirst for your blessing.
- I feel betrayed when you show yourself as human, so I turn on you and betray you.
- I defer excessively to authority I respect but hugely resist authority I do not respect.
- I secretly despise you and want to harm or steal from you. I agitate against you behind your back and attack you when your guard is down.

"Low self-esteem is the belief that we are not good or worthy enough. It's a self-perception. It doesn't matter how successful or confident you are. You can be wealthy, beautiful, or well-liked by others and still don't feel good about yourself. The way other people perceive you doesn't affect your self-esteem. It's how you perceive yourself that matters."
Yong Kang Chan

The Crumbling King Speaks

Each paragraph is the voice of a different man.

"I give up on myself. I fall apart. I utterly disintegrate. I am not part of this. I am collapsing, hollow, pretending. I am terrified of being seen, of being me."

"I'm hiding. I don't want the world to see me. I'm not good enough. I try, but I just can't pull my life together. The things I try to do don't work. I am a failure.
My self-doubt holds me in chains and stops me from stepping up. I feel ashamed of myself.
I believe my self-critic. I am subservient to you. I am small and insignificant.
You have all the power. I have no power."

"I'm confused, frozen, disconnected. I've let the side down. I'm just not wanted.
I've got nothing to contribute. I get in the way. I hold things back. I am a big black hole full of shit. I hold all the things that I can't do. I have a negative view of life. Life goes on but I am not in it. I am the dumping ground for all shit, all negativity, any disappointment, regret, all negativity is put on me.
I hold it because I don't have anywhere to put it. It sits with me in this dark corner of the kingdom. No one comes here. I don't care about myself. Sometimes I hurt myself."

"I'm waiting for permission, for the starting gun. I wonder when my life starts. I don't know if I'm allowed. I should just coast. I'm too old to start again. It's too late to make anything of myself."

"I don't have a voice. I'm scared of using my voice. I'm underconfident. I cower in a corner. I feel excluded, not loved."

"Here I dream all the bad things that are going to happen. I don't really sleep. This is my insomnia, my self-harm, my suicide attempts. It is a lot, a bottomless pit of darkness.
There is no light. It is just this way. There is no other way. This is how it is set up.
I suck up all the toxic mess. I am really, really tired. I basically want to die."

"I fix, rescue, and take care to cover my not good enough. I don't believe in myself.
I try to be something for other people, what I think they want me to be.
If I am myself, they might not like me. I do the extra thing to please others.
I'm not good enough. I can't change.
I don't feel like wearing a crown. I'm not worthy. I'm small. I keep my head down.
I can't be good enough. I get it wrong and get punished.
I defer to other kings. I need their approval and acknowledgement."

"If there is someone with a big ego, I slink into the corner and let them take centre stage. I become very introverted. I blame situations for me not stepping up. I get overwhelmed. I flap around like a headless chicken in a daze. I do nothing, but it takes a lot of energy. I can't play the sovereign, I want to go back into the womb, to go back into mother. I'm a ghost. I'm a grey man."

"I don't know my meaning or my purpose. I don't have any meaning.
What gifts do I have? I can't see any. I defer to authority I admire.
I hate and despise authority I don't admire.
My kingdom is in huge collapse. It's all burning down. I just can't look after myself anymore.

I don't want to take responsibility. I have so many superficial surface relationships. People aren't interested in me. I'm so unimportant and impotent. I'm pathetic and weak. There's just no point making any effort. I have no energy.
I've given up before I've started."

"I don't believe I'm good enough, ever. I feel small, beaten down, lost. I feel down, low. I don't know why I feel like this. I hate being so powerless. I hate myself. I've tried so many times and nothing works. I just want to disappear. I don't want to be here. I want it all to be over. It is too painful, too stressful.
Nobody cares."

The Tyrant King Archetype

Having met your Too Little King it is now time to swing to the other side of your Heart King and meet his second wounded brother, the Too Much King, the Tyrant Archetype.

We are dividing your Kings into 3 characters, but actually they are on a spectrum, with your Heart King as your middle ground, and your Tyrant as too much King energy, and your Crumbling King as too little King.

If we are wounded in our Sovereign we are likely to cycle between our Tyrant and our Crumbling King in a somewhat bipolar fashion. I long, long fall from inflated Tyrant all the way down to deflated Crumbling King. Our Tyrant tries so hard to stay on top, but when he overextends and messes up, he falls or collapses into his desperate Crumbling King. With great effort he finally pulls himself out of his collapse, only to sail past his Heart King back into his Tyrant.

The Tyrant King's effort is to cover up and hide his wounded beliefs from himself and the world. He tries to achieve this by being much, much better than these painful, shameful beliefs. However, no matter how great he is in the world and how successful, his happiness is hamstrung by his undermining idea of himself. This form of the King is very shaky indeed as he has no solid foundation on which to base himself.

As with the Crumbling King, we will have a look at how our Golden Boy was wounded so that he grew into this struggling King.

As a child, the boy learns that he is not loved or approved of for who he is as a unique person. He learns that his essence as a person is not important, and he is only welcome and accepted when he acts as his parent or caregiver demands. This is a significant blow, a painful wound to his sense of self. In his struggle our boy fights against these beliefs about himself:

Fighting Against the Belief:
- I am better than everyone else. I am entitled to privileges.
- I can just take and not give back. I should be able to do whatever I want. It doesn't matter what effect I have on others.
- I am superior, so I must have power and control.
- My sense of self depends on money, status, achievement, and appearance. I use these to gain approval, admiration and attention.
- Others should be harshly punished if they make a mistake.

With these beliefs firmly entrenched our wounded boy fights against his wound and manifests in adult life as the harsh, overbearing Tyrant King. As you did with your Crumbling King, you are about to recognise and get to know your Tyrant. Try to suspend your judgements and shame you feel about being like this. This is the time for your overbearing Tyrant to show himself so your Heart King can know his brother King and take him into account.

Read through the behaviours of this Tyrant King archetype and notice which you recognise in yourself. Take time with your perusal. Tap into the energetic field of this archetype. Feel into him for yourself. As you identify aspects of yourself in the outline you are reading, notice how your Tyrant King plays out in your life.

What other ways does this King show up in your thoughts and actions? This list of behaviours is here for you as a starting point, so you can recognise how the Tyrant King archetype behaves. In what other ways, not listed here, do you act as this King? Note them down to start building a picture of your Tyrant King.

Wounded Behaviour of the Tyrant Archetype

- I am the Tyrant King. All this is for me. I pursue the **Path of Power** over others and power for myself.
- I must be seen and admired. I am the King, or I am nothing.
- I am the self-obsessed high-chair Tyrant. I am infantile, vain, self-involved and self-serving.
- I love authority, influence and status.
- I am the law. I am the source of order. I am the state, the Kingdom.
- I fail to recognise that the greatness of the King belongs to the archetype. I think I am that greatness.
- I gain power so that I have control over everything.
- Because I am the best, I must get to the top and stay on top.
- I am a grandiose extrovert **narcissist**. I'm shining for approval. I perform for love, attention and praise. I deluge you with my extreme self-confidence.
- I have an overwhelming need for your admiration. I attract and monopolise your attention. I aim to impress you. I want to be important to you. Your attention makes me feel alive, whole and significant. Your focus must be on me.
- I am the centre of the universe. I am **special** and unique. I have a childish sense of my importance and power. I feel like a god.
- Only special unique people understand and appreciate me. You are not in my league if you don't see how great I am. You're not special.
- I inflate my talents and achievements. I seek positions of power to be admired and show you I am superior to you.
- I exhibit myself. I put on a great show of myself and want you to watch.
- I attempt to seduce you. I try to draw you under my thrall. Once I have enmeshed you, I am a nightmare to disengage from.
- I reward flattery and servility. I punish, humiliate and destroy anyone who opposes me. I undermine and thwart any sense of shared purpose. I model everyone being out for themselves.
- I am self-centred and greedy. I want material things, and I never have enough. I don't know when to stop.

- I constantly compare myself with others and rank myself higher than them. I am determined to be the best. My self-worth depends on it. I am jealous of and hate your success.
- I confuse myself with my job role. I think I am that role. I believe I am what I do.

> "The narcissistic orientation is one in which one experiences as real
> only that which exists within oneself,
> while the phenomena in the outside world have no reality in themselves,
> but are experienced only from the viewpoint
> of their being useful or dangerous to one."
> Erich Fromm

- I have a **strong sense of entitlement**. I need special treatment. I don't have to do anything to automatically get awards and adoration. You must comply with my expectations without question.
- I am superior to you. You must admire, glorify, honour, worship and bless me. You must acknowledge how superior and valuable I am.
- My loyalty is only to me. It is not to the company or my workers. I negotiate for myself. I will sell out the company if it benefits me, even if all those who depend on me lose out. I burn and destroy what I and others have created.
- **Believing deep down that I am not good enough** leaves me uncertain, fragmented and paranoid. I fear you have found me out, seen through me, and are waiting to turn against and destroy me.
- I am so uncertain about myself that I am defensively hostile to you. I take you out before you get a chance to betray me.
- Any beauty or flourishing life is an assault on me. I am irrational, paranoid and abusive.
- I hate and fear new life, brilliance or rising talent. It is a threat to me, and I attack it.

> "Narcissists are consumed with maintaining a shallow false self to others.
> They're emotionally crippled souls that are addicted to attention.
> Because of this they use a multitude of games,
> in order to receive adoration."
> Shannon L. Alder

- I **lack inner structure,** and despite my bluster, my internal belief system is weak. I have no sense of myself that I can love and rely on. I am insecure. I hold no centre, either in myself or in my world.

- I'm covering up that I believe at my core that I am worthless, corrupt, shameful and valueless. Much of my effort in the world to be significant is to hide this. I have to do something extraordinary to win your love and admiration, so I will see that you believe I have worth.
- I overextend myself due to my lack of discipline and become very scattered, which leaves me exhausted and distracted.
- I become even more dramatic and theatrical when I fear that people will see through me. If this does not work, I change friends and find a new arena to display myself to a different audience.
- I cannot stop and take stock. I am impulsive and impatient. I am motivated by my fear of being deprived or missing out.
- I am unaware of my heart's inner guidance, so I am unclear in my decision-making. I am anxious that my choices are wrong, especially since I never stop long enough to look inside. I push ahead anyway, even against the advice of others.
- With little inner guidance, I try everything to see what I like. This wasteful approach leaves me unnecessarily busy, so I become frustrated and make decisions that damage my health, work and relationships.
- I am always searching for something beyond my grasp. I dream about an impossible future. If I get what I want, I am disappointed by its reality, and so imagine a new object glittering in the future. The grass is always greener elsewhere.
- I am obsessed with **fantasie**s of unlimited success, power, and brilliance. If I'm not grandiose, I am depressed.
- You are here to magnify my status and celebrate my greatness and achievements.
- I meddle in your life and manipulate you to get my own needs met. I need to be put on a pedestal and adored. You must worship me. I bask in your admiration.
- I am so proud of myself. I believe in my PR, but I have no idea who I am and what controls me beneath the surface.
- I create conflict at work, so I have to change jobs and careers regularly.
- I deceive myself that I have no darkness inside me. I think I'm great, and that is all there is. I'm light and bright.

"From where I'm sitting,
I AM the centre of the Universe!"
Sebastyne Young

- I am a superhero. I'm **on fire.** I'm blazing. "I can do this. I can ace it".
- I am manically high. I'm uninhibited and say whatever comes into my mind. I am flamboyant, witty, jokey, and the "life of the party". I perform and love to be the centre of attention.
- I vainly exaggerate my achievements and talents so you admire me.
- I have so many new ideas and many incredible plans. I can't say "no". I throw myself into one activity after another. I don't discriminate between fruitful and unfruitful enterprises.

- I will care for you, save you, rescue you. I seduce you to control you. I turn against you if you assert your independence from me. I undermine you if you try to do things on your own.
- I am afraid of being bored. I want perpetual motion. I do so many things, but few of them well. I don't follow through and move on to the next project before completing the last one.
- I make irresponsible decisions that are risky or harmful. I suddenly spend lots of money or embark on another risky venture.
- I **talk non-stop**. I ramble, talk to stay in control, and hide my vulnerability.
- I lie. I am dishonest. I accuse others of being corrupt.
- I give mixed messages. I abuse others verbally. I gossip. I manipulate with words. I slander, denigrate, mock, harangue, and scold. My words create discord, strife and turbulence.
- I dominate with my voice. I interrupt. I yell, vocally attack, accuse, vehemently shame and wound.
- I do not want to listen to you. I can't wait for you to stop talking so I can turn the conversation back to myself.
- Talk about me. Talk about my achievements, my money, my greatness, and my success. Talk about how great I am.
- I don't want your inner truth, so I shut you down. There is only room for me, none for you.
- I **lack empathy**. I don't recognise or identify with your feelings or needs. I am unfeeling and impatient with your emotions.
- I have sacrificed my feelings on the altar of business and success. Emotions get in the way of profit. They have no value. Doing and thinking are far more important than feeling. Feelings reveal weakness.
- I no longer know what my emotions are. I try to do feelings, to feel what I think I am meant to feel.
- I struggle with intimacy. Others tell me they feel I am not real. I have an air of phoniness and inauthenticity. Like the Crumbling King, I suffer from Imposter Syndrome.
- I am terrified of failure.
- I am impatient, rude, snobbish, disdainful, arrogant and patronising. I am brutal, pitiless, ruthless and insensitive.

> "Often the narcissist believes that other people are "faking it",
> leveraging emotional displays to achieve a goal.
> He is convinced that their ostensible "feelings" are grounded in ulterior,
> non-emotional motives.
> He feels compelled to avoid emotion-tinged situations,
> or worse, experiences surges of almost uncontrollable aggression
> in the presence of expressed sentiments.
> They remind him how imperfect he is and how poorly equipped."
> Sam Vaknin

- I idealise and **project onto the feminine,** who I see as the perfect goddess. My view keeps her imprisoned, incarcerated, isolated and starved. I control her beautiful body, bringing it out occasionally to possess and penetrate.
- I hold the feminine out of life. On the one hand, I idealise her into perfection, keeping her high on a pedestal, so she's not real. I demonise her, on the other, as the devouring mother. I ensure that either way, she tears me to shreds.
- I see relationships as a contest for control. I use all the women in my life.
- I see sex as the place to acquire pleasure from the other.
- I rate my masculinity by the size of my biceps, my wallet, my penis, and my accomplishments.
- I marginalise, subjugate, betray and exclude other men. I fight to be the alpha male.
- I am the **Tyrant**. I control and abuse.
- I wage war to feel important and to increase my power and influence. I tyrannise to stay on top.
- If you are not for me, you are against me. If you are against me, I seek to disgracefully destroy you. I look for opportunities to block, banish, betray, undermine, hurt, accuse and sabotage you.
- I gather power for its own sake. I always hold the most powerful position. I will do anything to hold on to power.
- I break down and transgress your boundaries to show you that I am more powerful than you.
- I am full of pride and reckless overconfidence. I throw caution to the wind and lack prudence.
- I terrorise, murder, torture, beat up, intimidate, enslave and humiliate to control. I seek to ruin you. I break your resistance, your body and your spirit.
- The only way for you to survive is to comply with me.

> "The sadistic narcissist perceives himself as Godlike,
>
> ruthless and devoid of scruples, capricious and unfathomable,
>
> emotion-less and non-sexual, omniscient, omnipotent and omnipresent,
>
> a plague, a devastation, an inescapable verdict."
>
> Sam Vaknin

- I get people into **crisis mode** where strong emotions have much more effect.
- I project my internal drama outwards and catch others in the turmoil I create. I attract some and repulse others. People obsess about me, even when they are not around me. I lead people to extremes.
- I despise, banish, target and attack people in my group and those outside my group.
- I say there is an evil villain or a malicious, dangerous group out to get us.
- I put myself forward as the only one who can keep us safe. I use the drama I have created to justify why I should be in power.

- I use highly emotional media to get everyone worked up and on my side.
- I want you to follow and love me, so you do my bidding.

> "When one with honeyed words but evil mind
>
> persuades the mob,
>
> great woes befall the state."
>
> Euripides

- I denigrate, damn, diminish and chastise you, but hate you criticising me. I am intolerably sensitive and think you have no right to scold me.
- I easily fall into the Crumbling King with the slightest criticism and feel deflated and impotent. I don't want you to see this, so I rage and righteously attack you.
- Beneath my rage, I feel worthless, weak, ashamed, vulnerable and not good enough. If I cannot be the great King, I am nothing.
- If I sense any weakness in you, I attack you, so I do not feel the weakness in me.
- I am destructive. If I don't get my way, I abandon and destroy.
- I am divisive, sarcastic, suspicious, envious, scornful and disparaging. I instil fear.
- I am corrupt and can't be trusted. I am dangerous. I will make it look like it was you who fucked up.
- I get obsessive, vindictive and malicious. I will annihilate you if you remind me of my inadequacies and failings.

> "Hate is the complement of fear, and narcissists like being feared.
>
> It imbues them with an intoxicating sensation of omnipotence."
>
> Sam Vaknin

- You only exist to serve me. I see you as an extension of myself. I **use you**, then disgracefully abandon you. I exploit you to achieve my ends. You only exist to give me attention and validation. I devour you.
- I lure you in with flattery and attention, but this never lasts long, and soon I turn cold and hostile. I seduce and pull, and then I reject and hurt. I turn against friends. I control who is in and who is out. I don't have deep intimate relationships.
- I see you rising to success as a threat, and I do my best to block, subjugate and undermine you. There is no room for any Kingship apart from my own.
- I do not bless, praise or honour you. You are here to praise and honour me. You are here to magnify and glorify me.
- I am your saviour. You are nothing without me. You are lucky even to have a chance to associate with me. You are not worthy of me.

- In a relationship, I don't want you to give attention to anyone but me. I get you to cut contact with your family and friends.
- I am envious of you or believe you are jealous of me.
- I humiliate subordinates in front of other people.
- I pretend to hold the moral high ground. I am righteously outraged at injustice or others' failings, yet I mistreat others and have secrets and vices. I project my negative qualities onto others. I judge and condemn you. You are all good or all bad. I use rules and political correctness to damage you.
- I degrade beauty, talent, innocence and all life-giving energy. I demean and disdain my sons and daughters, killing their hope and life force. I ignore their skills, success and accomplishments.
- I over-punish and under-praise. I physically abuse the masculine and beat my sons. I sexually exploit the feminine and harm my daughters and the earth.

"This work was strictly voluntary,
but any animal who absented himself from it
would have his rations reduced by half."
George Orwell, Animal Farm

- I am right. I am the expert. I disagree with you, and I make sure you can't be right or prove me wrong.

The Tyrant King Speaks

Each paragraph is the voice of a different man.

"I have drive. I push, and I roar forwards. I am going to fucking make this happen. Anyway, your way of doing things is not good enough. I push you back. I drive over you. I am a dragon. I burn you up."

"I am an arrogant bastard. I walk over everyone to get to the top. I smash others up who get in my way. I don't let any other cunt get a word in. Pay attention to me. Listen to what I say."

"If you don't pay full attention to me, I will fucking hurt you. If you do not do exactly what I want, I will destroy you. I will pick you apart, because you are incompetent and useless."

"Do it my way, or you are wrong and bad. I am an authority figure. I have authority over you. You will do as I say. You are nothing. I am the despot. I am alone, ruthless. I am the centre of the world. This power is delicious."

"I put people down. I'm a right cunt. I say "get the fuck out of my way". These fucking idiots that get in my way, can't they see I'm on a fucking mission? I see the target. I'm coming through."

"I leave a wasteland behind. You talk about engaging, empowering. Fuck off! I'll get it done. It's me against everyone. It's either black or white. I fight the universe. I carve a path upstream. I go against the flow. I am so strong. I let everyone know you are talking shit. I walk away because you have nothing for me. I love watching you fail and fall apart."

"I don't consult. I don't share. I don't reign in my passion and energy. I make it your fault if I hurt you. I batter you with the force of my words. How can you not see how I'm right? I don't need help from anyone else. I like being in control."

"You're incompetent. You don't know what you are doing. My way is the only way. I can't be bothered with you, waiting for you is a waste of time. Any way other than my way won't work. Do it my way or shut up. I want to usurp you. I want to take you down. Fuck you. I want to lead to boost my ego. Obey me because I am better than you."

"I tell people what to do. I have a very clear idea, and I get it done. I just keep asking until I get my way. I will make sure it's done, my way. Woe betides you if you get in my way. I'm rude and short with people. I'm arrogant. I'm powerful. This power is delicious."

"I step in. I take over. I run everything. I don't pussyfoot around. I don't fuck around. Call on me. I know what I'm doing. I know what needs doing. I don't need to work out what needs doing. I already know. I like it when people fail. Then I can step in. No-one does it better than me."

"I lack finesse. I'm careless. People get hurt. That's tough. Its collateral damage. I don't get relationships. I ride roughshod, waving the flag of victory."

"I don't learn. I don't adapt. I have no empathy. I have grandiose ideas, but I'm holding back because you cannot handle what I have to give. I want to be on top."

"My thinking is all or nothing. I behave in extreme ways. My emotions are out of control. I target people. I want unlimited power."

"I get people into crisis mode where emotions have more effect. I say there is an evil villain. Then I say I am the only one who can keep people safe. I attack people in the group. I dominate, and my Predator destroys. I use high emotions and the media to shape opinion. I talk, I talk, I talk, I talk, I talk, I talk, and I talk some more. I want you to love me so you will do my bidding. I have an authoritarian personality."

Part 3

The Magician

Introduction to The Magician Archetype

"Do not grow old, no matter how long you live.
Never cease to stand like curious children before the Great Mystery
into which we were born."
Albert Einstein

Now that you have got to know your King and his two wounded brothers, it is time for your Heart King to get to know your Magician.

Rene Descartes' quote "I think therefore I am" sums up the Magician and how he functions. The Magician is the thinking part of ourselves, and he makes himself known in our minds.

Our Magician contributes a vast amount to our Kingdom, but even he needs the guidance of his Healthy Sovereign to mature, evolve and function in the best way. As his King's adviser, he needs to work closely with his King to function at his most balanced and effective.

Our Magician manifests as the inner dialogue in our heads. As with all other internal characters, our Magician needs his King's boundaries and guidance; otherwise, we have to live with his endless thought conversation that never stops.

Our Magician lives in the world of our mind by creating and managing our thoughts. His existence is dependent on our mind. When his thoughts stop, he is not active.

Our Magician attempts to monitor our local environment. His effort is to understand our world and keep it under control. He gains an impression of what is going on, and he then tries to make inner mental sense of our outer world. With his mind, he makes judgements and considers various ideas. He takes the form he sees in the world and makes it into an energy pattern in our mind that he can interpret and manipulate.

"You have to take seriously the notion that understanding the universe
is your responsibility,
because the only understanding of the universe that will be useful to you
is your own understanding."
Terence McKenna

Our Magician sees everything going on, but he mainly focuses on what means something to himself. He thinks through what matters and processes it to match with his particular model of reality. He makes a mental model of the world he sees.

Most of what our Magician sees makes no particular impression and so passes straight through. Our Magician experiences then releases, so he is ready for the next moment. He is alert, prepared and present, flowing and integrating with life.

It is important to remember that your Magician interprets the world according to the mental model you build up over time. The reality you are creating is your own personal view, not necessarily the actual reality that exists. You have recreated the outer world in your inner mind. Your Magician's personal view is your self-fulfilling prophecy. Your mindset shapes the reality you perceive. It is the lens through which you view the world.

Your Magician interprets and processes your current experiences in a way that conforms with your views and your mental model. Doing this gives you a feeling of sanity and control. It means that you protect your view of the world and feel stable and secure.

Your Magician's perception comes from a number of factors, including:

- Your genetic make-up.
- The voices and attitudes of your parents, authority figures and society that you internalised when you were young.
- Painful and traumatic experiences that had a negative limiting effect on you.

Your Magician's deepest longing is to trust. He wants to believe that he understands and has done enough so that he can leave life to unfold in its own particular way without him having to control every part of it. He wants to find a place of equilibrium so that his mental system can settle, observe, learn, and make minor adjustments.

> "The important thing is not to stop questioning.
> Curiosity has its own reason for existing.
> One cannot help but be in awe when he contemplates the mysteries of eternity, of life, of the marvellous structure of reality.
> It is enough if one tries merely to comprehend a little of this mystery every day.
> Never lose a holy curiosity."
> Albert Einstein

When your Magician is not in equilibrium, he thinks a lot to try and work out his problems and confusion. His thinking releases some of his discomforts, giving him the impression that he is more in control. He thinks his way through a problem as his way of working it out and integrating it.

Your Magician stays in his flow, at ease with his world and all in it, until something happens that he is not happy about. His concern causes his flow to stop. Instead of moving on to the next moment, he sticks with the impression that upsets him. He fixes on it even though the event that brought it about has gone. It doesn't flow through him but jams up and becomes an unfinished experience that now lives on within him.

Your Magician moves on but now has an obstruction within himself. This unprocessed event, now a blockage, doesn't just sit quietly. It needs processing to bring it to healing completion so it can dissolve and pass through. It comes to his mind regularly seeking release. He thinks about it often.

The more events that have jammed in your Magician, the more blocks will call to him for healing, and so the more active his mind will be. Some unhealed, unfinished events may stay in his mind for a very long time.

As we know from physics, energy must move. If an event cannot heal and flow out of your energy field, then your Magician will keep circling the block in his mind. In time, he may build equilibrium based on his mind endlessly circling several long-established familiar blockages.

> "The doors to the world of the wild Self are few but precious.
> If you have a deep scar, that is a door,
> if you have an old, old story, that is a door.
> If you love the sky and the water
> so much you almost cannot bear it, that is a door.
> If you yearn for a deeper life, a full life, a sane life, that is a door."
> Clarissa Pinkola Estes

It takes up a lot of magician energy to maintain a holding pattern around these blockages. The energy you have available for the rest of your life is decreased. In time, if some of these blocks are not cleared, your life force will be severely reduced. Not much energy is moving in, and little is passing out. Your Magician becomes bogged down and depressed. What little is moving in and out is affected by the blocked energy and so takes on a negative slant.

Each of these energy blocks inside your Magician is a live energetic force. Each holds the actual event that caused it and all the pain and hurt of that event. This event was not processed; it continues to live as if it is still real and happening, even though it may have happened a long time ago. The event is still operating and felt as underground sadness, anger or fear. You may no longer connect these moods with the blocks that live within you, but they directly spring from your unprocessed inner blockages.

To make matters worse, these blocks don't just stir up background moods and unhappiness. When you encounter a new event that resembles a past painful blocked event, your original pain is activated, as well as a fresh wound to add to it. You are infused with your first pain and a new level of hurt that piles on top of it.

> "Every one of us gladly turns away from his problems, if possible,
> they must not be mentioned, or better still, their existence is denied.
> We wish to make our lives simple, certain, and smooth,
> and for that reason problems are taboo.
> We want to have certainties and no doubts – results and no experiments – without even
> seeing that certainties can arise only through doubt
> and results only through experiment.
> The artful denial of a problem will not produce conviction;
> on the contrary, a wider and higher consciousness is required
> to give us the certainty and clarity we need."
> C.G. Jung

Your healthy, wise Magician is the part of you that seeks to know you inside out. Therefore, it is his job to highlight these blocks so that your Sovereign can attend to each block, process and heal them, and integrate them into his heart. When he does this, your energy can flow freely within your system again.

Your King's job is to work with his Magician to bring peace and healing to all in his realm. To do this, your King needs to differentiate and separate himself from his Magician. He can do this by stepping back from his Magician's thoughts and watching them from a distance. He can learn to observe and notice his thinking rather than believe that he is this inner voice. His effort is not to think about his thoughts, as thinking is his Magician's job, but just to notice them.

Separating your King from his Magician means that your King is the one who notices what his Magician is thinking. He is aware of the thoughts in his mind and knows that he is not these thoughts but is the one who hears them. Your King is the one who witnesses thinking rather than the one who is doing the thinking. He does not get lost in thought. He observes how his Magician thinks things through. He makes a separation between himself and his Magician, and he knows who is who.

> "The planet has a kind of intelligence,
> that it can actually open a channel of communication
> with an individual human being.
> The message that nature sends is:
> transform your language through a synergy between opposite forces
> ~ a synergy between dance and idea ~
> a synergy between understanding and intuition,
> and dissolve the boundaries that your culture has sanctioned between you."
> Terence McKenna

In some sense, the whole of our civilised world originates in the Magician. He thinks of something first and so creates it in his mind. As a Healthy Magician, he offers his creative options to the King and advises him as to their workings and merits. It is then up to the King to choose which option to bring into being. After this, the Warrior, who protects and supports the King, swings into action according to his King's orders. The Warrior now gives body and reality to the Magician's imaginings and brings the King's choice into being.

The Magician within us all is actively pushing forward the two arms of his being. He is responsible for the tremendous technological surge that is transforming our world. He is also responsible for humanity's deepening turn inwards as men and women seek to evolve, heal and mature before our increasingly imperilled planet collapses under its human strain.

> "When you beautify your mind, you beautify your world.
> You learn to see differently.
> In what seemed like dead situations,
> secret possibilities and invitations begin to open before you.
> In old suffering that held you long paralysed, you find new keys.
> When your mind awakens,
> your life comes alive and the creative adventure of your soul takes off.
> Passion and compassion become your new companions.
> As St. Iraneus said in the 2nd Century,
> "The glory of God is the human person fully alive."
> John O'Donohue

The Healthy Magician Archetype

Read through the Healthy Magician Archetype behaviour below and notice and note which you recognize in yourself. Take time with your perusal. Tap into the energetic field of this archetype. Feel into him for yourself.

Identifying certain aspects of your Magician in the outline, feel into this archetype as it plays out in your life. What other ways does your intelligent Magician show up in your behaviours? How do you behave as your Magician?

Write up all of the Magician aspects that apply to you until you feel you have a good picture of yourself as your Magician.

Remember that this portrayal is the Archetypal Healthy Magician at his best. No one manages to embody all of this Ideal Magician.

Behaviours of the Healthy Magician Archetype

- I exercise the power of my **mind**. I embrace both the verifiable data and the unknown, the invisible and the mystery.
- I am a **thinker**. I think, therefore, I am. I am cerebral.
- My mind is my tool. I use it for rational analysis. I understand and respond through my intellect, through ideas. I want intellectual order.
- I am the shaman, the psychologist, and the scientist. I operate in so many professions in the modern world that need my mental agility and bright intelligence.
- I am the **elder, the wise old man**, the spiritual guide, the **shaman**, the sorcerer, the medicine man, the psychotherapist, the priest, and the guide to individuation.

> "Through our eyes, the Universe is perceiving itself.
> Through our ears, the Universe is listening to its harmonies.
> We are the witnesses through which
> the Universe becomes conscious of itself."
>
> Alan Watts

- My specialism is accessing and transmitting sacred and esoteric knowledge and power. I understand the laws of nature and the fundamental ways of the human psyche. Most of all, I know my intimate inner world.
- As a priest, I am religious, and I work with established religious structures and ceremonies.
- As a spiritualist, I am engaged in ecstatic communion with the divine.
- I encourage transformation, healing, and evolution.

- I am highly independent and focused. I live to an extent in my own world, slightly apart from the community. Despite this, mine is a social role, and I need to be used in my community.
- I am a shaman. I know that the origins of modern knowledge and technology lie with our age-old ancestors. I feel my roots in tribal and ancient societies. I bring the power of the spirit world to my community.

> "The small man builds cages for everyone he knows,
>
> while the sage,
>
> who has to duck his head when the moon is low,
>
> keeps dropping keys all night long for the beautiful, rowdy prisoners."
>
> Hafiz

- My shamanistic aspect may have been born in illness, a traumatic life crisis, or severe psychological disruption. At some time, I may have learned my craft by falling apart and slowly putting myself back together.
- I am so **interested**, so curious. I love to become engrossed in whatever I am fascinated by.
- I want to find out how things work, how the world ticks. I am curious and continuously seeking deeper understanding.
- I am always asking questions, searching for new knowledge, and looking for hidden depths.
- I am interested in change and in establishing new pathways in my brain. I know that to create a new path in my brain, I must repeat a novel action 400 times. I also know that I can also achieve this change by repeating a new step 14 times in play.
- I choose not to close my mind to something, even if I don't agree with it or don't like it. I have no limits in my thinking. I constantly search for new ideas and novel ways of thinking. I embrace my childlike spirit and my I original curiosity.
- I want my ideas to be challenged, so I search for knowledge in all cultures and times. I set free all my creative powers.
- I **don't just accept established opinions** or wisdom. I need to understand for myself. I like to test accepted thought to see if what others believe is true.

> "The important thing is not to stop questioning.
>
> Curiosity has its own reason for existing.
>
> One cannot help but be in awe when he contemplates
>
> the mysteries of eternity, of life, of the marvellous structure of reality.
>
> It is enough if one tries merely to comprehend a little of this mystery every day.
>
> Never lose a holy curiosity."
>
> Albert Einstein

- I love having interesting original thoughts and ideas. I often say insightful and unusual things.
- I don't want to explore what is already known. I am not interested in the familiar and well-established.
- If you agree with my opinions too readily, I worry that my ideas are too conventional.
- I try to overturn established ways of thinking.

> *"Normality is a paved road:*
> *It's comfortable to walk,*
> *but no flowers grow on it."*
> Vincent van Gogh

- You can **rely on me**. I am responsible and dependable. I am trustworthy, mature and controlled. My actions are deliberated and deliberate.
- I think before I act. I am patient. I am aware of how my emotions move me, and I take into account how they affect my ideas and decisions.
- I think through all possible consequences of my plans. I resist my tendency to be blind to potential risks. I sceptically and prudently reassess my strategy and continually look for new solutions and wider options.
- I build and hold a rational, pragmatic structure.
- I am good at foreseeing problems. I am also good at troubleshooting. I love to find solutions and fix glitches.
- Being somewhat detached, I don't take sides and so help to foster cooperation.

<u>**Skills:**</u>

- I **balance my logical thinking with my psychic** abilities.
- My **logical**, rational left-brain mind thinks in pieces, following from one piece to the next until I synthesize the whole from the parts.
- I am a master of technology. I create transformation in the material world. I can see into systems and evolve them into technologies that serve.
- I am analytical by nature. I read volumes of information to ensure my facts are correct, and then I verify them again. I aim to "trust, but verify".

> *"It is easier to perceive error than to find truth,*
> *for the former lies on the surface and is easily seen,*
> *while the latter lies in the depth,*
> *where few are willing to search for it."*
> Johann Wolfgang von Goethe

- My right brain manifests my **psychic** intuition, which acts as a flash of light in the dark, where, in one moment, I see the entire picture.
- I am holistic, imaginative, intuitive, mentally flexible and introspective, and good at seeing different angles.
- I deal with the unseen world and with hidden knowledge. I am at home in the supernatural, the secretive and the mysterious.
- I am the observer. I am the archetype of **self-awareness**. I examine myself and my life to know who I am, to see my patterns, my true nature, and to be authentic. I work out how to be who I truly am. I work out what in myself is holding me back.
- I am thoughtful and aware. I reflect and seek insight.
- I perceive. I cut through my illusion to understand myself. I seek out what I do not know about myself. I search for my shadowy places. I find out what golden shadows I have formed so I can reclaim my gold.

> "Better keep yourself clean and bright;
> you are the window through which you must see the world."
> George Bernard Shaw

- I ask myself, who am I, what is the meaning of my life, what is my vocation, where am I going, and what is the purpose of my life?
- I bring guidance to my Sovereign by raising, deepening and widening my awareness.
- I am measured. I keep my ego in check. I keep an eye on my grandiosity and keep myself in balance. I check when I am in denial or pretending. I keep myself balanced with the other archetypes.
- I notice what I get worked up about in others. I accept that there is something about myself in my reaction.
- I am the initiator, creating and holding **transformational and initiatory space.**
- I am the student, the teacher, and the master.
- I create the container for transformation to occur and facilitate this transformation. I hold the boundaries of sacred space.

> "I have been and still am a seeker,
> but I have ceased to question stars and books;
> I have begun to listen to the teaching my blood whispers to me."
> Hermann Hesse

- I steward initiatory and spiritual space, which I separate from the ordinary profane world and connect to the universe's eternal fabric. The sacred space I create has an Axis Mundi, a holy tree leading to the centre of the earth and the heavens.

- I rejuvenate individuals and society by creating regenerative and transformational energy. I initiate into greater wisdom, into a more developed rounded human existence.
- I am the mentor who guides the initiate from the ordinary world to the 'other' world where transformation can occur.
- I am a **communicator**. I synthesise new ideas and original metaphors and communicate them to the world from multiple perspectives. I translate old wisdom in a new way, and I disseminate information.
- I am a teacher. I advise and inform. I make connections with my wisdom. I love to simplify complicated concepts and expose them to new audiences.
- I love puzzles. I like to follow clues.

> "Only he who can see the invisible can do the impossible."
> Frank Gaines

- I hold the overview, the macro picture.
- I love to delve into the tiny details, to explore the micro.
- When asked a question, I think for a moment to commit to the question and answer before I answer.
- I am the **Safety Officer**. I am orientated towards security.
- I decide which parts of myself to work with and which to put into shadow. I keep parts of myself that I judge are unsafe out of sight and try to keep them out of action.
- The virtue I hold is that of prudence. I never rush into a project but will always research precisely and adequately.
- I don't react; I respond. I am always present in a crisis. I am here to watch out in case of threats. I look out for problems and alert my King.
- I detach from the immediate rush of events and create perspective. Stepping back, I look at the broader context. I consider the immediate against my long-term aims. I take time to gain information and discern the truth.

> "It is important that you draw wisdom from different places.
> If you take it from only one place it becomes rigid and stale."
> Iroh.

- I usually play out possibilities in my mind before I allow any action. I stay detached from the heat of the moment. I dig deep and wide to look into the future as a way of limiting my attraction to short-term thinking and immediate, instant gratification.
- It is hugely important for me to be correct, and my worst fear is to be proven wrong.
- I **work closely with my fear**. I do not run or hide from it.
- I sit with my fear and make sense of what it is indicating. I learn from it where the danger is and what could go wrong.

- I make adjustments depending on the message in my fear.
- I know my **inner darkness**. I know that my animal nature has been active since the beginning of time.

> "Though my soul may set in darkness,
> it will rise in perfect light;
> I have loved the stars too fondly to be fearful of the night."
> Sarah Williams

- I watch out for this deeply instinctual part of myself, so I know when I want to predate on myself or others. I know how dangerous I can be.

Gifts:

- I am **the strategist, the planner, and the organizer**. I am objective and work in the background to make sure everything works properly.
- I work out what is going to happen before the action takes place. When the action does occur, I fine-tune again. I plan the road ahead and make sure we stay on it.
- I build a model and check it works properly. My model provides structure and order.
- I prepare properly. I practice. I gather all the resources I am going to need.
- I study so that I genuinely know what I am going to be doing. I make sure I have mastered the correct techniques.
- I assemble information to reveal **patterns**, and then I work out what the pattern meant in the past and what it may mean for the present and the future.
- Each time I recognize a pattern, I integrate it and move towards wholeness, a bigger picture. I shatter my illusions, develop clarity and depth, and move to a broad vision.

> "The highest form of human intelligence
> is to observe yourself without judgment."
> Krishnamurti

- I am **on a quest**. I belong to creation. I bring into being what was not there before. I am a co-creator within the universe and am involved in a constant process of re-creation.
- I explore the world of ideas. I seek and study hidden philosophies and sacred and secret knowledge.
- I have had contact with the numinous. I am looking for a magus to guide me. I search to find this guidance deep inside myself. In an initiation, I will find it within transformative space where my old, limited being can die to be reborn as more wholly human.

- My foremost power is my **imagination**. I am **inventive**. I see the world in my way, differently from everyone else. Some think this makes me strange, but I am ahead of others, ahead of my time. I am a **visionary**.

> "Two roads diverged in a wood, and I—
> I took the one less travelled by,
> And that has made all the difference."
> Robert Frost

- I am a **dreamer**. I dream for inspiration and ideas. As a dreamer, I am also a storyteller. I imagine new worlds and creative narratives.
- I investigate out-of-the-way places, the bizarre, the secret, areas where others would not think to go. I explore the far reaches, beyond the usual, into unknown territory.
- I want to know what others know nothing about and create something no one has ever experienced before.
- I love to be an expert in my particular niche.
- I make new pioneering discoveries because I look at things in entirely new ways.

> "You cannot swim for new horizons
> until you have the courage to lose sight of the shore."
> William Faulkner

- I **concentrate**. I **focus** so that I can develop complex ideas and valuable skills.
- I am intensely focused on my particular area of interest. I am a master of that which has captured my interest. Nothing escapes my notice.
- I practice my skill to achieve mastery. I am disciplined.
- I have so many **qualities** that are useful in my kingdom.
- I am mentally alert. I pay attention. Because I pay attention, I am profoundly **perceptive** and insightful.
- Not only do I understand the wider world, but I also skilfully penetrate its individual mysteries.
- I love to see into the future and predict what is going to happen.

> "The significant problems we face cannot be solved
> at the same level of thinking we were at when we created them."
> Albert Einstein

The Magician Speaks

Each paragraph is the voice of a different man.

"I'm the thinker. I'm rational. I step in to create a better situation. I create transformation. I uncover beauty and reveal all the good things. I create lots of good ideas. I am not attached to them. I love to hear other ideas."

"I'm ok. You're ok. This world is ok. I can see, hear and feel it. I can analyse to know this world is ok. I have great ideas. My imagination is really powerful. I can see and determine when the quality is high. I see the bigger picture. I am connected with it all. I am intuitive and perceptive. I am fascinated by detail, by how the world works. Knowing all this is my form of love, my gift of understanding the mystery of life, and the beauty of our interconnection."

"I work step by step. I break down small problems into smaller problems. I am the observer. I see patterns. I am measured and thoughtful. I am not quick to act. I contain myself. I look out for problems. I anticipate them. I am good at troubleshooting. I don't take sides. I am always willing to change my mind. I feed my curiosity by looking into things."

"I know how things should be done. I bring huge insight. I strategise. I've kept the kingdom safe. I bring great gifts of understanding and intuition. I love to keep busy. I feel calm and stable, working with my king. I bring strategy and power."

"I bring a lot to the king. A sense of spirituality collated from all over the world. I have hunted and gathered from many spiritual kingdoms. I have tracked many wisdom keepers. I have captured wisdom with my magical devices, and made them available to all the kingdom, and to many other realms.
I know technology. I can strategise out of dark holes. I can communicate with tyrants and bullies with compassion.
I can channel predator and safety officer.
I see the positive and the negative. I see behind the masks. I have a great imagination. I am creative. I have skills in many of the arts. I inspire with knowledge. I draw on many lifetimes of knowledge and experience, that I gained from many thousands of years living on this planet. I have a strong, quiet voice that can warn you when things are getting out of control.
I am faithful and loyal. I know death. I am not afraid of death.
I know failure. I am a healer. I use energy to cast out darkness.
I recognise when I'm relevant and when another archetype is required.
Then I step aside.
I see the invisible and the hidden."

"It's up to me to figure things out. I figure out how things work. I understand and fix. I use my magic to order the kingdom. I take things apart until there is nothing left."

"I am deeply soulful. I am connected to life in good ways. I can go to dark ways safely. I love ritual. I love daily routines. I know there are darker aspects to my being. I am their equal."

"I am the higher voice outside him. Detached. Speaking from the outside. Still, separate from the drama. I am not affected by the physical plane."

"I know how to trust, this is what I truly long for at all times. Everything I do is about finding trust, the trust that who and what I am fits in with the world. That trust allows me to be still and quiet, when I am still and quiet my intuition and insight is extraordinary. I can bring in information beyond the logic I am so good at when I am still and quiet. Then my council is truly wise."

The Manipulator Archetype
Too Much Magician

*"I feel like a defective model,
like I came off the assembly line flat-out fucked
and my parents should have taken me back for repairs
before the warranty ran out."*
E. Wurtzel

Now you have met and made a relationship with your Healthy Magician, it is time to meet and know your wounded Magician parts that struggle with unhealthy behaviours. These Magicians believe that something is wrong with them, that the world is unsafe, and they are faulty, defective, and bad. They either manifest as Too Much Magician, who works very hard to be safe while hiding his defects, or become Too Little Magician, who has given in to his belief that he is defective and maybe evil and can do nothing about it.

We will start looking at these two wounded Magicians by trying to understand how a Magical Boy can be wounded. Having understood this, we will look first at the Too Much Magician, the Manipulator.

How a Magical Boy is Wounded

As with your Sovereign Boy, your Magical Boy had particular essential needs as a child, so he could grow up feeling safe and accepted.

These included:

- being understood,
- being held in safety,
- being able to trust,
- having opportunities to develop his intelligence,
- being given space to be different,
- being allowed room to experiment with himself.

If these needs are not met, he loses trust in the world and himself. Listed below are some of the actions and family experiences that may have wounded him.

Wounding family actions and events:

- Cheating, lying to and manipulating the boy.
- Demanding perfection, criticising, and punishing his mistakes.
- Belittling him, calling him stupid or idiotic.
- Not encouraging him or denying him schooling, disparaging learning.
- Attacking his emotions.
- Enforcing unnecessary rule-following, unexpectedly changing the rules, making erratic demands of him.

- Encouraging him to be cruel to animals and people.
- Teaching him to be a bigot, racist, and sexist.
- Encouraging him to steal and break the law, asking him to sell or supply drugs.
- Modelling being fearful, pessimistic, and catastrophic.
- Demanding that he study excessively.

Resulting Beliefs

In the face of this relentless damage to his Magician sense of himself and the world, the boy may give up and accept that he is less than, that he cannot be himself, that he is not safe, and that there is something badly wrong with him. Or, instead of giving up, he may fight against these painful, wounding beliefs and try way too hard to prove them wrong.

In reality, he probably swings in a bipolar fashion between giving in to these beliefs and fighting against them.

Fighting Against his Beliefs:

- I must cheat people because they will try to cheat me.
- I must manipulate to evade people who are planning to use me and get control over me.
- Something is wrong with me. If people knew, no one would love me.
- I am flawed, wrong, and defective. Maybe I am evil, dark and sinister.
- I am ashamed of my flaws. I must hide them. I must hide who I am.
- I am going to go crazy. I am fracturing, falling apart, and breaking up.
- I must meet rigid rules of behaviour. My health, happiness, and peace are not important compared to meeting these rules.
- I focus on the negative. I obsess over all the mistakes I have made, all the loss, betrayal, and disappointment. I complain constantly.
- Something is going to go seriously wrong, and then everything will fall apart.

Fighting against these undermining childhood beliefs, the wounded Magical Boy grows into your adult Magician with Too Much Magician essence. I have called him the Manipulator. He uses his mind and tries to manipulate his world to stay safe and hide what he believes about himself from a dangerous world.

As you did with previous archetypes, read through the behaviours of the Manipulator, and notice and note which you recognise in yourself. Take time with your perusal. Tap into the energetic field of this archetype. Feel into him for yourself. Recognising certain aspects of yourself in the outline you are reading, feel into this archetype as it plays out in your life.

What other ways does this clever Magician show up in your behaviours? How do you behave as your Manipulator? This list of behaviours is here for you as a starting point, so you can recognise how the Manipulator acts. What are the other ways, not listed here, that you behave as a Manipulator?

Wounded Behaviour of the Manipulator Archetype

- I have **too much mind**, too many visions. I am preoccupied with obsessive fantasies, delusions, imaginary constructs, and even hallucinations.
- I am excess Magician at the expense of other areas. I lack grounding, and I have little connection to my body.
- I can't quiet my mind and let it settle. It loops endlessly through the infinite realms of my imagination. I can't stop thinking.
- I continuously imagine better alternative realities and so dwell on the past and the future.

"You can't get away from yourself.
You can't decide not to see yourself anymore.
You can't decide to turn off the noise in yourself."
Jay Asher

- I am **preoccupied with logic and intellect.**
- I am trying to work it all out, get all the answers right now, fix my life, have all the solutions, and solve the future.
- I remember everything I have learned and carry it around in my head.
- I collect facts. I am always looking out for more information and adding to my collection.
- I am a **perfectionist**. My perfectionism is based on my fear and shame. I try to protect myself from judgment and blame by using the perfect shield of being completely correct.
- I am so determined to be perfect that I struggle to start or complete a task.
- I hold myself back to make sure that what I say will be perfect. I endlessly think through everything I want to say before I express myself perfectly.
- It will be a catastrophe if things aren't perfect.

"Perfectionism is the unparalleled defence for emotionally abandoned children.
Perfectionism provides a sense of meaning and direction
for the powerless and unsupported child.
In the guise of self-control,
striving to be perfect offers a simulacrum of a sense of control."
Pete Walker

- I **guard against looking too deep within**. I am scared of looking at myself as I fear I am evil. I don't want to accept that about myself.
- I display myself as spiritually advanced while glossing over and hiding all about myself that I don't like and do not want the world to know.
- Though I will not see the darkness inside myself, I am pleased to point it out in you. I tell you what you need to do to evolve yourself.
- I am **controlling**. I can't delegate work to others unless they submit to doing it exactly as I want it done.
- I am obsessive and compulsive. I am preoccupied with orderliness and with controlling my mind and myself. I need everything in its particular place and under my control.
- I need rules and established procedures to dictate the correct answer to me. Without them, I have far too many options, and this is painful. I am preoccupied with lists, details, order, organisation, and schedules.
- I use rules and procedures in dogmatic ways to control. I am rigid and inhuman in my insistence that people must stick to unnecessary, heartless rules.
- I am over-conscientious and over-scrupulous.
- My morals, values, and ethics are inflexible.

> "Control and manipulation are not love;
> the outcome is a life of imprisonment
> ultimately leading to deep-rooted feelings of resentment."
> Ken Poirot

- My **safety officer is too strong** and has me tied up in knots. He imprisons me. He is deeply risk averse.
- I am always running protective strategies to survive, such as being invisible, hyper-vigilant, trying to control all of life, and being a people-pleaser, a perfectionist, and a chameleon.
- My safety officer manufactures excess fear and anxiety to stop me from doing anything risky and keep me small and safe. I worry constantly, can't sleep properly, have trouble breathing, and sweat too much. I have a range of phobias and stomach issues.
- I have panic attacks. I panic. I feel fearfully disordered and short of breath. My heart pounds. I tremble and shake and feel like I am choking. I have pain in my chest, feel dizzy, feel detached from myself, and wonder if I am losing control, going crazy, or dying.
- I create a sterile world in which I stay safe. I want clean, secure, predictable technology to control the world.
- I struggle to confide in people, or to reveal my true self, even to friends.
- I find it very difficult to trust. I believe others will try to use me or take advantage.
- I believe others are dangerous and might betray me. I always watch out for this.

- I see danger in many everyday situations, threats that others don't notice.

> "Life is made of fear.
> Some people eat fear soup three times a day.
> Some people eat fear soup all the meals there are.
> I eat it sometimes.
> When they bring me fear soup to eat, I try not to eat it, I try to send it back.
> But sometimes I'm too afraid to and have to eat it anyway."
> Martin Amis

- I am **difficult to get along with** and often have problems with close relationships. I participate in everyday life, but not in society.
- I am suspicious, hostile, argumentative, sarcastic, complaining or hostilely aloof.
- I struggle to function in society. I have a borderline personality disorder. I turn away from social attachments. I don't trust anyone. I am incredibly self-sufficient. I try to control you. I can't collaborate or accept feedback or leadership.
- I can be eccentric. I am told I am weird.
- I don't like challenges to my views and become abrasive, cynical and argumentative when others question my extreme and radical opinions.
- I won't confide in you in case you use this information against me.
- I bear grudges and am unforgiving of insults, injuries or slights.
- I see attacks made on my character or reputation that others don't notice. I am quick to counterattack.
- I create discord in groups by gossiping, undermining, trying to destabilise leaders, getting others to take sides, creating cliques, criticising, and rallying support to my side.
- I take up all the space in groups. My process is so colossal. Everyone is dragged into it. I make sure the group twirls around my orbit.
- I am committed to my pain. I work on it relentlessly, but I never heal. Everyone knows my painful wounds. They know what was done to me.

> "I feel like a defective model,
> like I came off the assembly line flat-out fucked
> and my parents should have taken me back for repairs
> before the warranty ran out."
> E. Wurtzel

- I don't understand or see the point of emotions. I see **emotions as a weakness**.

- My lack of feeling means I do not develop lasting close friendships or relationships. I turn to interests that are more rewarding to me than people. I prefer to tinker with things.
- I lack eros. I stay away from relationships. I find them messy, painful and distracting.
- I keep emotionally distant. I have no idea what love is.
- I use others' emotions to gain an advantage over them. I pretend to be helping them while alienating and isolating them and making them dependent on me.
- I **habitually lie**. I trick you into believing my lies.
- I lie to myself. I am full of self-delusion.
- If someone catches my lie, I continue to lie despite the evidence. If I cannot lie my way out, I attack.

> "The Manipulator portrays himself as a victim of circumstance
> or of someone else's behaviour
> in order to gain pity, sympathy or evoke compassion
> and thereby get something from another."
> George K. Simon Jr

- Even though I may seem detached, I am **highly strung and intense.**
- I have powerful emotions. When my feelings are intense, I melt down and fall apart over small things.
- I have mood swings that last for hours or days. At times my mood changes dramatically.
- I operate on a thin line between **insanity and genius**. I am at home in the borderlands, in the nether regions, beyond the pale, outside the borders.
- I get lost in the offbeat, in the dark and disturbing, the esoteric.
- I become obsessed with imaginary worlds and detach from reality.
- When I get obsessed with darkness, I end up becoming terrified of the world. I skew into distortion and disorder.

> " Do not look for my heart any more;
> the beasts have eaten it."
> Charles Baudelaire

- I have **psychotic** episodes. I am attracted to killing myself. I seem to be deranged, schizophrenic, and self-destructive.
- I am agitated by hallucinations. I see, smell, taste, hear and even see things that are not real.

- I become deluded. I develop unshakeable beliefs in things that are not true. I believe I have powers. I am convinced my delusions are real.
- I stumble over words, talk relentlessly and fast, lose my thread, branch off into unrelated areas, gabble and talk incoherently.
- I struggle with stress-related paranoid thoughts and severe dissociative symptoms.

> "Dearest, I feel certain that I am going mad again.
> I feel we can't go through another of those terrible times.
> And I shan't recover this time.
> I begin to hear voices, and I can't concentrate.
> So I am doing what seems the best thing to do."
> Virginia Woolf

- I use my **shadow shamanic power** not to guide others but to manipulate them in ways they cannot see.
- I believe **I'm 'bad'**. I isolate myself to protect people from me.
- I am not interested in helping others but want to use my knowledge to influence and manipulate them. I damage my students.
- I control, use, and abuse others to maintain my power, advantage, status, and success.
- I seek to destroy. I am the trickster. I demolish good men. I delight in their destruction. I do not want to replace them. I want to defeat and annihilate them.

> "I am terrified by this dark thing that sleeps in me."
> Sylvia Plath.

- **I exploit the earth and all other forms of life.**
- The natural world is here for me to use. I have no feelings for the earth or animals.
- I work out how to consume the resources of the natural world to my benefit. I wring every last profit out of it. I deplete, exhaust, and destroy.
- I do not care about the damage I cause. My machines extract all that is of value and then move on to find more, leaving a wasteland behind.
- I am the arch manipulator. I **predate** on others and act like a vampire. I am the dark Magician, controlling, manipulating, deceiving and 'evil'.
- I feel shame. I feel ashamed because I believe that 'I'm bad'. I attempt to keep my shame at bay by self-monitoring and excessive self-scrutiny. I work hard to prevent my flawed self from showing.
- If I am not predating on others, I am predating on myself. I am the self-critic. I am cruel to and persecute myself. I am the remorseless judge and the critic of myself. I believe in all my self-criticisms. I corrode my world by filling myself with shame.

- I persecute and humiliate, sowing hatred, intimidation, separation, and envy.
- I distrust others and am suspicious of them. I believe their motives are suspect or even evil.

> "Every step closer to my soul excites the scornful laughter of my devils,
> those cowardly ear-whisperers and poison-mixers."
> C.G. Jung

- I assume you want to exploit, harm or deceive me, even if I have no evidence to support this. I believe it because I think you must be like me, and I want to exploit, manipulate, harm and deceive you.
- I am hyper-vigilant for potential threats; guarded, secretive, devious, cold and lacking in tender feelings.
- I am sexually manipulative. I won't admit this, even to myself. I harass sexually. I obtain sex in abusive ways. When accused, I react with indignant protestations of innocence.

> "The fish looks eagerly at the red fly
> With which the fisherman will take him:
> But he does not see the hook-
> So it is with the poison of the world,
> Its danger is not realised."
> Mechthild of Magdeburg

The Manipulator Speaks

Each paragraph is the voice of a different man.

"There must be a right, perfect way. I try to control every detail. I'm rigid. I like lists. I overuse logical structures. I come up with endless ideas, far too many. With so much data, I get lost in thought.
I have put up a perfect shield to protect myself. If it doesn't work, I will kill myself.
I have no feelings for my family or friends. I am a freak, deformed, one of a kind, abnormal, different. I need to be right all the time. I can't bear to be wrong. I can't bear to make mistakes. I can't bear to be challenged around anything. How dare you think you know more than me.
I naturally lie. I use lying as a tool, even when I don't need to. It's my way of hiding and protecting myself. I lie and manipulate to make sure I am seen as special, the smartest, the most intuitive, the cleverest.
I am threatened by other magicians.
If they seem cleverer than me, I judge them mercilessly."

"I go away into fantasy, sex, porn, my phone, drink. I dissolve into numbness – tunnel out. You don't need to do this. Just run away. Escape reality. Check out. I am off in a dream world. I'm eccentric and weird. I am a controlling perfectionist. Lists, details. I come up with 10,000 options and stick you in option paralysis."

"I feel unaffected by anything. I feel centred, safe and powerful when disconnected from the entire world, from my entire world.
I hide when I get depressed. It's safe here, a spiritual place, the place I go when I meditate. There is nothing here, but I am self-contained, and this saved me. I hold grief, my youngest part, in my belly. I could spend most of my life here, in a cave, alone, not having to connect with anybody.
Every possibility is open to me, and I choose not to take any of them. My safety officer is fucking active. He has a foot on me, holding me down. Making sure I can't get up and connect. He is in control. He had to be so strong to suppress me so I could survive, so me, in some form could survive.
I've got my little boy in here with me. I keep him surrounded, hidden and safe. No one can get to him, or my grief. I can't feel my grief. I have it so well protected.
I'm numb. I numb my lover boy, so he's safe, but he's not allowed to express."

"I know I'm bad, I find it easy to hurt others in an underhand way. I can gossip and talk behind peoples' backs, knowing it will hurt them. But I don't care. Somehow, I want people to know that I'm bad, cruel and evil. It's a bit of a cry for help, but no-one can help me, I'm too far gone, broken and ashamed."

"It doesn't matter what you say to me, I will always have a cleverer, more potent and powerful answer. I have to be bigger, better, smarter, more sure of myself. Most of the things that come out of my mouth are statements or judgements, I am rarely curious or interested in anyone else's point of view, they can't have any value. If you challenge me, I will destroy you with my intellect."

"I am often paralysed by fear. I will overthink and overthink some more. I'm so scared of getting it 'wrong' that I will procrastinate for eternity before making a decision. In fact, I won't get to the decision at all, I will delay so long, analyse every possibility, every nuance until an outcome is forced upon me, then I am a victim."

The Dummy Archetype
Too Little Magician

"Do you know that feeling? When everything you do seems like a struggle.
Where you don't wanna leave the house
because you know everyone is judging you.
Where you can't even ask for directions in fear that they criticise you.
Where everyone always seems to be picking out your flaws.
That feeling where you feel so damn sick for no reason.
Do you know that feeling where you look in the mirror
and completely hate what you see?"
Anonymous.

As your Heart King, you have become familiar with your Manipulator, one side of your wounded Magician. Now you have an opportunity to understand yourself as the Too Little Magician, the Dummy.

Like your Manipulator, your Dummy suffered from a wounding childhood where your core needs were not satisfied, so you could not develop a sense of being safe and accepted in the world.

Your core needs were the same as those listed for your Manipulator, and you were wounded by family actions just as your Manipulator was. Unlike your Manipulator, who fought against these wounding beliefs, you gave into them and so came to believe certain things about yourself.

<u>Giving in to these Beliefs</u>

- I am stupid. I can't understand.
- I can't solve my problems. I can't work out what's going on.
- Catastrophe is about to land on me. I am so afraid because I know I won't be able to do anything about it. The world will destroy me.
- I am so afraid I will make mistakes that will ruin and humiliate me.
- I must maintain incredibly high standards, or I will get criticised. I must be very critical of myself to keep my performance up.
- I must pay infinite attention to detail, be efficient, and always be on time. If not, I will get in trouble.
- I am chronically worried. I have to watch out all the time. The world is not safe for me.
- I will only survive if I am totally rational and disregard my emotions. I must control and hide my feelings.

Believing all this as a child and teenager, he grows into your Dummy Magician.

Read through the behaviours of the Dummy archetype and notice and note which you recognise in yourself. Take time with your perusal. Tap into the energetic field of this archetype. Feel into him for yourself. Recognising certain aspects of yourself in the outline you are reading, feel into this archetype as it plays out in your life.

What other ways does this Dummy show up in your behaviours? How do you behave as your Dummy? This list of behaviours is here for you as a starting point, so you can recognise how the Dummy behaves. What are the other ways, not listed here, that you behave as a Dummy?

Write up all of the Dummy that applies to you until you feel you have a pretty good picture of yourself as your Dummy.

Wounded Behaviour of the Dummy Archetype

- I **lack self-awareness** and consciousness. I live my life but don't try to work out what life is about, or its meaning.
- I don't have a strong sense of who I am. My understanding of myself changes depending on who I am around.
- I am childishly and naively innocent. I have repressed and hidden my cunning and manipulation from myself and the world. My innocence is a pretence.
- I won't look within. I will not own up to the truth about myself. I claim not to understand my behaviour, my relationships, or my place in the world.
- I project manipulation onto others. I believe I am only good. I cannot see darkness in myself.

"Every one of us gladly turns away from his problems,

if possible, they must not be mentioned, or better still, their existence is denied. We wish to make our lives simple, certain, and smooth,

and for that reason problems are taboo.

We want to have certainties and no doubts – results and no experiments – without even seeing that certainties can arise only through doubt

and results only through experiment.

The artful denial of a problem will not produce conviction;

on the contrary, a wider and higher consciousness is required

to give us the certainty and clarity we need."

C.G. Jung

- I **don't organise** my life. I do not make plans. I do not look into the future.
- I am not investigating anything. I have no interests. I am bored.
- Life stretches ahead of me as a void. The future holds no possibilities for me. It will be the same as it is now.
- I am unstructured, unplanned, chaotic and undisciplined.
- I can't think outside the box, have **no imagination**, and have trouble thinking of something I haven't already seen somewhere before or something not proved.
- I can't imagine behaving differently. I can't imagine change.

- I believe what I believe, and nothing will change my mind. I am narrow-minded. I do not question what I believe. I don't want others to challenge it either.
- I am afraid that I'm **stupid**. I don't **understand**. I'm confused.
- I can't function successfully in the world. I hide, keeping secret and elusive.
- I am over-loyal to ideas and beliefs that have had their time. I don't question the status quo. I fight for these beliefs much more strongly than is sensible.
- Rejecting my inner shaman, I project it onto others who I judge to be spiritual. I need others to hold sacred, initiatory space for me. I cannot evolve myself or anyone else. I am not capable of mentoring or teaching.
- I **can't concentrate** or focus. I am constantly distracted.
- I don't have any area of expertise. I have not developed any new thoughts or unearthed any unusual information.
- I have so many scattered thoughts that I never do anything.
- I shun success. I couldn't cope with it. I don't complete my projects. To finish or be successful would expose me and make me afraid.

> "I'm an expert on stupid.
> I can spot stupidity, because I know it so well.
> The way an exterminator knows bugs really well,
> and can spot where they've been?
> I'm like that. A stupidinator."
> Brandon Sanderson

- I **don't remember**. I can't evolve as I soon forget any change I have made. I can't hold on to any growth or new behaviour.
- I have checked out of parts of myself. I hide from the parts of myself I do not like.
- I am **fragmented, scattered and confused**. I have no confidence in my mind or in my judgement. I appear to be ignorant.
- I have too many points of view and take on everyone else's opinions. I need you to think, to work it out for me.
- I have only one point of view and one identity. I constantly say, "I know". I stifle others' opinions. If my one point of view is shattered, I fall apart.
- I have no point of view. I constantly say, "I don't know". I can't see the other side and won't expand into the unknown. I am rigid, dense, and stifled.

> "I learned how to stop crying.
> I learned how to hide inside of myself.
> I learned how to be somebody else.
> I learned how to be cold and numb."
> Sherman Alexie

- I am cold, detached and unemotional.
- I am **numb** because I decided not to endure my feelings, and I closed them down.
- I am limited in the emotions I express. I have no emotional depth.
- If I express affection, I am highly controlled and stilted. I am very uncomfortable if you are emotionally expressive. I give the impression I don't care about anyone or anything.
- I am formal and serious and very stiff around happy people.
- Your praise or criticism does not affect me.
- I am **isolated**. I don't want to be around people. I avoid socialising and don't create or maintain strong personal relationships.
- I don't care about other people. I prefer friendships with animals.
- I like solitary activities. I prefer to work alone or in a job where I don't have to be around people.
- My strange way of speaking and my odd mannerisms make it difficult for me to hold a normal conversation.
- I can't attend to my imagination and maintain relationships at the same time. It is one or the other.

"We're all islands shouting lies to each other across seas of misunderstanding."
Rudyard Kipling

- I am so **anxious**. I am so desperate to feel secure.
- I am afraid that I will be 'found out' when you see what an awful person I am. I am so scared that you will then reject, ridicule and shame me.
- I see the world as a dangerous place. I watch out for hidden motives and harmful intentions. I don't feel safe.
- I am filled with unspecific anxiety. Something is wrong or about to go wrong, and I don't know what it is. I have a nameless sense of dread that I can't shake off. If only life were reliable and clear-cut, maybe everything would make sense and be safe.
- Because I am scared, I am overcautious. I can't make decisions.
- I think that you are going to make me wrong. I react to everything you say and defiantly try to make you wrong.
- Please guide me. I can't direct or support myself.

*"I wish to weep
but sorrow is
stupid.
I wish to believe
but belief is a
graveyard."*
Charles Bukowski

- I am a **nihilist**. I reject religious and moral principles. Life is meaningless. Nothing is real. Why try? It's all hopeless.
- I am **negative**, cynical and pessimistic. I prefer to sit on the side lines and criticise and knock down your efforts.
- My profound negativity is passive-aggressive. I use it to deny all responsibility for my life and to knock others down to my level.
- I don't trust leaders. I am suspicious of authority. I fear that leaders will manipulate me.
- I always feel others judge and blame me.
- I hide my true self and feel that I can never be honest.
- I always feel like the bad guy.

> "A pessimist is a man who thinks everybody
> is as nasty as himself,
> and hates them for it."
> George Bernard Shaw

The Dummy Speaks

Each paragraph is the voice of a different man.

"I'm a dummy. I struggle to understand. I have a really poor memory. I don't think before I act. I am incapable of planning. I love it if others plan for me. I follow others' advice. My head is full of cotton wool. I hate reading. I fucking hate it. I don't want to know. If I don't plan, I have an 'out' for when it goes wrong. I forget what I mean to say. I forget names."

"I am utterly lost and confused. I have no idea. I am frozen. I am nervous, hiding, anxious. I can't process what's going on. I can hear, but it makes no sense. I can't perform. I'm stuck. I grasp at ideas, and immediately and completely forget them.
What am I supposed to be doing here?
I'm so stuck. This is so familiar. I'm mind fucked, numb."

"I wing it. I just run with it. I'm not good at planning, organizing. My safety officer is in total control. I get blocked around simple words. I live life as it comes day to day. I don't see the darkness in others. I don't see it coming. I'm a thought thief. I take others' opinions. I surround myself with people who have similar thoughts. I don't question what I believe. I don't ask myself why. I find it very difficult to focus and concentrate. I drift off. I lack feeling. I've locked that door. I hear it in my head. But it doesn't move me."

"I can't step into the unknown. I won't step in if I don't know the outcome. There is something wrong with me. I don't trust myself. I keep away from the world outside. I play the innocent. I'm fragmented, scattered and confused. I am untethered, with no plan or structure. I don't organize my life. I can't look into the future. I'm unemotional. I value control, the formal. I am self-critical."

"I can't think. I can't think how to do it. I can't make a decision. I won't make the right one. I need to disassociate, watch porn, play on my phone. I disassociate. I'm so afraid. I distract myself. I close down. I'm mind-fucked, disorientated. I'm afraid of getting it wrong. I'm in paralysis. I check out. It's impossible to find the truth. I'm stupid, a failure."

"I like to follow rules, be a part of a system or organisation that means I don't have to work anything out, I can follow the rules set down by others and not have to think. It makes me feel safe, so I love working in law or admin or something deeply bureaucratic. I won't do problem-solving at all, that's way too dangerous and my mind just won't go there."

"I don't believe in anything beyond the rational, all this spirituality, shamanic stuff doesn't make sense to me, I don't trust it. I prefer to stick to simple, down-to-earth tasks, where it's as simple as going from A to B. Life doesn't have some amazing meaning, we are just insignificant motes in the vastness of space, those that think otherwise are deluding themselves. It's their desperate attempt to have some meaning that none of us have."

"I feel anxious most of the time, whenever I am around others I feel sure they are going to see how stupid I am. My mind doesn't seem to work in the same way as theirs, they make all these connections and have amazing imaginations and I just don't get it at all. It makes me feel so dumb and stupid, then I just get more anxious."

The Safety Officer Archetype

"You can play it safe, and I wouldn't blame you for it.
You can continue as you've been doing,
and you'll survive,
but is that what you want?
Is that enough?"
J.M. Darhower

Introduction

You will now have a chance to meet your Safety Officer. It is vital for your Heart King to be aware of this part because our Safety Officer usually has huge power and effect in his Kingdom.

We all have a part of us that tried to keep us safe. I have called him our Safety Officer. He usually came on board very early in our life and sought to protect us in the bewildering and uncertain world we grew up in.

As children, we had little power or agency. We were cared for by adults who had all the authority. To manage our small position in our enormous world, we needed our Safety Officer to help us watch out for difficulty and danger. This part sought to get us to fit in so that we received the love and protection we needed to thrive as children.

Our Safety Officer's job was to scan our environment to spot threats, difficulties or danger so that he would know what was needed to keep us safe and loved. As children, our Safety Officer worked out various risk-reducing actions that worked best. He regularly activated these strategies until, in time, they became our automatic, unconscious functioning. We moved into adult life with a set of protective tactics that our Safety Officer instigates whenever we face a difficult situation. Most of the time, we operate these strategies without being aware of what we are doing.

The main channel of communication that our Safety Officer uses to alert us to danger is fear. He administers fear so that we know we are in a risky situation and so we assess what is going on and take action to move back to safety. If we have not evolved our Safety Officer, he gets us to automatically instigate one or several of his favourite protective strategies that hopefully make us safe again.

"If we stay where we are, where we're stuck,
where we're comfortable and safe,
we die there.
We become like mushrooms, living in the dark, with poop up to our chins.
If you want to know only what you already know, you're dying.
You're saying: Leave me alone; I don't mind this little rathole.
It's warm and dry.
Really, it's fine."
Anne Lamott

Here are some strategies used by Safety Officers to keep us small, hidden and safe:
- Gets us to freeze in the face of perceived danger.
- Gets us to run away when we are afraid.
- Fills us with constant fear so we won't take any risks.
- Suffuses us with a feeling of background doom that we can't understand or change, which keeps us stuck and inactive.
- Makes us forget what we have agreed to do, so we don't change or evolve.
- Fills our mind with confusion, so we can't understand.
- Stops us from feeling and keeps our heart closed (feelings could get us hurt).
- Keeps us out of close relationships, so we don't get hurt.
- Gets us to close our heart, withdraw inside and hide away behind our shield.
- Gets us to close down our life energy so we are not too sensitive or receptive.
- Makes sure we don't try to change because change is risky.
- Gets us to research endlessly, so we never take action. Despite our constant research, our Safety Officer tells us we still do not know enough.
- Gets us to be a chameleon, so we stay camouflaged and do not expose ourselves.
- Gets us to fit in with everyone else and not stand out or be ourselves.
- Gets us to be the pleaser so we don't upset anyone.
- Keeps us insecure, stuck, and stagnant because it's safe and familiar.
- Stops us from feeling excited, enthusiastic or joyful.
- Makes sure we avoid conflict as this may be dangerous.
- Stops us from committing or taking action.
- Tells us there is something wrong with us, and we can't evolve.
- Gets us to hide the parts of ourselves that are weak or vulnerable.
- Tells us the world is dark and dangerous and threatening and that we always have to struggle to survive.
- Gets us to hide from the world.

> "When nothing new can get in, that's death.
> When oxygen can't find a way in, you die.
> But new is scary, and new can be disappointing, and confusing
> - we had this all figured out, and now we don't."
> Anne Lamott

- Makes sure we do not take a risk or face the exposure of being successful by sabotaging our success or making sure we do not complete our projects.
- Tells us we can't make mistakes and must be perfect.
- Keeps us in our head so we cannot feel.
- Makes us ill, so we cannot function or risk improving our situation.

- Gets our Inner Critic to fill us with guilt and shame to keep us small so we won't take risks.

As I mentioned, the primary tool used by our Safety Officer to communicate to us that we in a difficult situation is fear. Unfortunately, many men, including myself, were heavily encouraged as children not to feel or show fear. We were conditioned to believe that if we were feeling afraid, then we were cowardly. Conditioning like this means that as adults, it is challenging for us to engage healthily with our safekeeping, fear-administering Safety Officer.

If I have been conditioned not to feel fear, then one of two things happen:

1. I am not able to hear my Safety Officer. I suppress him, which means that I have no early warning system. The part of me which is supposed to alert me to danger is inactive. Because of this, I am likely not to notice when I am in danger, so I walk blindly into risky situations.

2. Because I do not notice when my Safety Officer tries to warn me with low levels of appropriate fear, he ramps up my anxiety until it reaches such high levels that I have to notice it. If I habitually ignore fear, then my Safety Officer batters me with more and more fear so that, in the end, he submerges me in toxic levels of unhealthy fear.

Until I know my Safety Officer, I will not easily pick up the fear he administers as an early warning system. I also do not know when I am unconsciously running one of his survival strategies. Unless I can see him clearly, I cannot evolve and upgrade him.

For most of us however an overactive Safety Officer is much more common. This parts ties us in knots and stops us evolving and maturing because change is dangerous and it is safer to stay as we are.

Now that you know the many strategies Safety Officers employ to keep us safe, have a look at the Healthy Safety Officer, and the Overactive and Underactive Safety Officers to assess how your Safety Officer is operating.

Healthy Safety Officer

> *"To overcome fear,*
> *here's all you have to do:*
> *realise the fear is there,*
> *and do the action you fear anyway."*
> Peter McWilliams

My Safety Officer manages my ancient survival programme, and it is his job to use his instincts and intuition to detect danger. This wise part of me wants to quickly find the truth in any situation to convey this truth to his King. A Healthy Safety Officer trusts that his King will hear him clearly by picking up the messages in the fear he is administering. He trusts that his King will take appropriate action to deal with risk when he understands the truth that his Safety officer is trying to convey to him.

If Safety Officer's relationship with his King is conscious, then when he administers fear, his King becomes fully engaged and assesses the fear to know the danger he is facing. He then decides to take appropriate action or press on if he feels 'safe enough'.

The Safety Officer's fear gifts the King with a burst of energy so that he is mentally alert and focused enough to prepare himself for the coming difficulty. Hopefully, it gives his King time to slow down and gather himself to be clear about the nature of the threat and gather the resources he needs to deal with it. As the Safety Officer's relationship with risk and danger is more intense than his King's, and because he doesn't have the same broad outlook on the kingdom as his King, his King may choose to accept the level of risk and go ahead anyway.

The vital thing to note here is that the Safety Officer is not responsible for taking action or implementing his strategies. He is only responsible for alerting his King, who then makes all decisions regarding what action to take.

An unevolved Safety Officer is very likely to be operating in an Exaggerated way or is Ineffective and Inactive.

Overactive Safety Officer

> "Of all the liars in the world,
>
> Sometimes the worst
>
> Are our own fears."
>
> Rudyard Kipling

An over-active Safety Officer tries to control the world by creating and maintaining safety. This approach would seem to make us safe, but actually, it makes the outside world seem more threatening than it is. He has to work so hard to keep the world functioning according to his design. He is endlessly challenged by a changing world so that in time he sees himself as pitted against a dangerous world in which his life is a great struggle. To stay safe, he has to make an exhausting relentless effort to force the world to be as he wants it.

This Safety Officer believes that life is not unfolding in a way that supports him. He sees his past as troubling and painful and his future as full of potential danger and problems. He does not accept that his life is okay as it is and so tries to work out how life should be, so he can force it to be that particular way.

An overactive Safety Officer lives a life full of fear because he does not trust that life will unfold in the right way. He is scared that life will threaten and hurt him, so he tries to control everything to reduce the risks of this happening.

An over-fearful, unevolved Safety Officer keeps us stuck in place with little room to manoeuvre, evolve or change. He tries to keep us away from our wounds because they are painful and because facing them is risky. To try to change is scary, especially if it means peering into our dark, hurting interior. Until he is evolved, our Safety Officer prefers what he knows and tries to keep going with his old-established strategies. Even when he sees that his efforts keep his King unhappy, trapped and hidden, he believes that he is doing a good job because he keeps us safe.

If my Safety Officer is too strong, I continuously run many of the strategies listed above. Because of this, I live a life where:

- I am in constant cycles of worry and anxiety.
- My fear clouds my vision instead of increasing my focus and clarity.
- I am not able to effectively deal with worrying situations, and so become even more afraid.

- I am overtaken, immobilised and overwhelmed by terror or panic.
- I lose my appetite and do not sleep well as I wake up and worry.
- Being afraid disrupts my reasoning, so I jump into a course of action without thinking things through.
- I experience Insomnia, uncontrolled shaking, fainting, and tics.
- I suffer from panic attacks, phobias, and depression.
- I try to protect myself by withdrawing from others.
- I try to cope by withdrawing from life.
- I cannot evolve or change and stay stuck in the same painful cycles.
- I resort to drugs, food and alcohol to try and cope with my fear. I find that this numbs my anxiety at times, and at other times it exaggerates it.
- I smell of fear so that I emit body odour and have cold sweats and clammy hands. I look pale and ill.
- I often freeze and find that I cannot do anything to help myself.
- I find myself breathing too fast, gasping, or holding my breath and gulping.
- My voice is shrill or too quiet. I stutter and mispronounce words. My voice trembles, and at times I struggle to speak up.
- I shake, feel dizzy, and lose strength in my legs.
- I become hypersensitive to touch. My adrenaline regularly spikes.
- I often want to flee or hide.
- I feel that everything is moving too fast. My sense of time becomes skewed.

Inactive Safety Officer

> "I'd felt the pop of the needle sliding into my veins, like a fang into flesh.
> I'd been enveloped in the golden haze where nothing is wrong
> even when everything is falling apart.
> A dance with a hypodermic fiend,
> my hands in the claws of a vulture."
> Taylor Rhodes

If my Safety Officer is half asleep, then I will have little safe keeping prudent function. I am likely to exhibit some of the following behaviours:
- I frequently demonstrate fearlessness in the face of danger, which leads me into damaging or unnecessarily dare-devilish behaviour.
- I throw myself into risky situations without preparation, study, or an understanding of the risks involved.
- I endanger my body and mind for no good reason.

- I do not honour healthy fear in others. I ridicule their fear and tell them just to be brave or get over it.
- I mask my fear with anger.
- Because I deny my fear, I turn away from it and do not understand its cause.

As I mentioned earlier, if I wish to evolve it is vital that I know this part of myself. On the Sovereign's Journey retreat our Heart King works with this Magician part to evolve it so that it functions in a way that suits our Sovereign.

The Safety Officer Speaks
Each paragraph is the voice of a different man.

"I don't want conflict, confrontation, and a war of words. I want it just to go smoothly. I am scared to stand up as I might not get it right. I won't stand up unless I know I can get it perfect, or more than perfect, truly excellent."

"We don't do messy. Messy is not appropriate. I keep control. Even if we give the impression of doing messiness, I make sure that it is controlled messiness."

"If he tries to step up, I get in his head. I distract him with thoughts that have nothing to do with what is going on. I take him to fantasyland, to dream places where he is safe.
I distract him with sexual thoughts at the most inappropriate times. I get him to go out and party. I distract him with another target. I get him to overthink things.
I get him so he can hardly string a sentence together. I leave him thick-tongued and stumbling. If he gets something wrong, I try and prevent him from being at fault.
I will say it was not his fault. I am economical with the truth.
To make sure he avoids being vulnerable or shamed."

"I don't want him to have a relationship. He goes hell pell forward. He flings his heart open. I can't have that. It's too dangerous."

"I am Safety Officer. I am happy to be here. I am not in the shadows. I am involved in everything. I love being able to do my thing. I watch out for things that could put him in danger. I let him know the people and places to avoid.
I keep his head down so he does not put it above the parapet.
I keep him camouflaged, unseen, invisible, not taking sides or risks. I keep him in confusion. I tell him more research is needed, that he needs to ask more people for advice, but I won't let him reach a conclusion. I let him have ideas but will not let him follow through on them in case he faces failure or ridicule.
I get him to please, to be nice, to take care of others.
I make him avoid conflict, to only be with people he can get along with.
If he overrides me, he will get it wrong.
If he does overrule me and goes ahead and gets it wrong, I call in Predator, who calls him stupid, a fucking idiot who has made such a stupid fucking mistake, who has caused it to all go wrong.
Then he won't overrule me again."

"I am the part that keeps us safe. I am clever. The more I know, the more I observe, the safer we will be.
I know all outcomes. I never close doors, never commit. I keep options open so that I can get out. I am a chameleon. If I'm not on the ball, I will be abandoned, destroyed, not wanted."

"There is something wrong. Something is different. Fight or fly from this impending doom. Something is really wrong. Something is really dark. The world is really dark. Everyone is dark. Humans are evil, and they're out to get me. I invest this fear in everything I look at.
I know something is going badly wrong."

"You need to be safe to exist. Don't get too hot or too hungry. Don't over commit.
Make sure you have enough sleep. Don't show yourself if you're not safe."

"I actually like his King, but he's stupid. At times he believes he's a King, acts like a King.
I have to pull the brake hard. He nearly takes off as King. He will make a laughing stock of himself. It is nothing. It doesn't generate money.
Although he feels happy and joyful, it's an illusion.
I keep him grounded and earning."

"Being the protector is a demanding job. I'm always available. I'm generally running the show. I need to always be ready to shut down the infiltration of feelings.
Feelings can kill; it could all be over."

"I use mental ideas, analysing, interpreting. I look to provide evidence of safety.
I fill him with fear to keep him safe by forcing him to avoid risks and by avoiding strong feelings.
It's worked so far.
But I know I am too much."

The Predator Archetype

Pred a tor

noun \ˈpre-də-tər, -ˌtȯr\

: an animal that lives by killing and eating other animals: an animal that preys on other animals.

: a person who looks for other people in order to use, control, or harm them in some way.

> "You not only are hunted by others, you unknowingly hunt yourself."
> Dejan Stojanovic

Introduction to the Predator Protector

Now it is time for our Heart King to descend even deeper into our underworld. We are entering an area of masculine behaviour that affects all our worlds. This is a challenging place to gaze, and to spend time in this arena takes courage and honesty. Please read my notes on Trauma in Appendix 1 if you have concerns about looking at this inner character, or if you have significant trauma.

For a man to have any chance of being at peace, it is essential for his Heart King to be aware of this wild, primal part of himself. On my Retreats your Heart King would work to acknowledge, love, integrate and repurpose this part. We can't do that here, so we will just seek for your Heart King to know and become as fully aware of how this part operates in you.

> "The ultimate objective of spirituality
> is not to remove the existence of evil or humanity's negative traits.
> Instead, we must confront and transform these dark forces,
> for it is only through the struggle of transformation
> that we ignite the spark of divinity within us."
> The Zohar

We all have this wild, naturally attuned, powerful and alert Protector; however, it is our early life conditions that determine how it functions in our adult life. We can see how a healthy protector operates by looking at predators in the wild, those animals that hunt and kill for survival. They live according to the laws of nature, which are "red in tooth and claw". In nature, this energy kills to survive but is not malignant, heartless or cruel. If we had a reasonably safe, benevolent childhood, our Protector was not called on to protect us and is somewhat benign.

If our childhood was not safe, and we were not protected from harm, our Protector would have risen to keep us safe. The degree to which we were abused, assaulted, neglected, or predated on as a child or a teenager determines the level to which our own protector/predator becomes activated and develops his power. When we were predated on as a young person, we did not have the power to stop the abuse. Our Warrior was smaller and weaker than our abuser or abusive situation and could not protect us and stop what was happening.

In response to the threat, abuse, and danger, another part, our Protector Predator, stepped up to protect us and help us survive the situation. With its incredible primal power, this wild, feral, animal side of our nature stepped in as the only force that could manage what was going on. This intelligent, devious, primeval, cunning Protector sought to help us to do whatever was necessary to survive, live, and possibly gain revenge another day.

If we were predated on as a child, we had innocence-destroying darkness forced upon us. Because of this, our Protector darkens into a Predator who reflects the abuse, danger, and trauma we endured. Once we escape the original damaging situation, we are often ashamed of this dark part of ourselves and seek to hide it from the world and, if possible, ourselves.

> "We all have a Monster within;
> the difference is in degree, not in kind."
> Douglas Preston

Many men are deeply troubled by this part, a part we judge as dark, evil, and threatening to those around us, even dangerous for those who love us. From this Predator, we get our Magician wound, which convinces us that we are dark, wrong, unlovable, and maybe even dangerous and evil. We go to great lengths to hide this part of ourselves but still feel it coursing below our surface.

Feeling there is something badly wrong inside, we try to hide our Predator from the world. We feel ashamed about being this way. In shame, we turn against this part of ourselves that once sought to protect us. We think we are vile and unacceptable, so we must hide our inner darkness. We deny our former Protector a loved and honoured place in our heart. We try to shove it into our dark, hidden depths where it cannot be seen.

When we turn against our Protector, it turns against us.

> "The inner critic,
> A heartlessly negative self-appraisal
> That originates in childhood,
> Who waggles its finger in our face
> So often that it's shaming of us becomes normalised.
> This internal drill sergeant,
> This love-barren, relentless inner overseer,
> Wears us down through self-castigation,
> Even as it pushes us to be better,
> To be more successful, to be more of a man."
> Robert Masters

When our Protector turns against us, it becomes our Inner Critic. It knows our every weakness, all our failures, insecurities and shortfalls. It had great teachers, those who it once tried to protect us from. It uses the words, gestures and abusive cut-downs of our former tormentors. It seeks to torment us and undermine every happiness or success we bring to our world.

Our Inner Critic self-predator can be extremely cruel, heartless, condemning and damming. His big stick is shame, and he administers it relentlessly. He pours shame on the parts of ourselves we are ashamed of, our lonely, misfit Lover, our ineffective, weak Warrior, and our abdicating, crumbling King. Sadly, these parts of us see the truth in his shaming words and believe his poison.

It is excruciating to live with an overactive, critical, self-predating inner enemy. It is even worse when this part of us teams up with our Safety Officer, as we can get stuck in a dreadful place where both will work to keep us small and stop us from evolving.

> "If the delivery of such internalised self-shaming
>
> Is sufficiently harsh,
>
> We may lose much or all of our drive,
>
> To better ourselves,
>
> Sinking into depression, apathy, and self-loathing,
>
> As long as we leave our inner critic unquestioned and in charge."
>
> Robert Masters

Do We Face or Hide from our Darkness?

Facing your Predator is an advanced piece of work for any Heart King. Instinctively we want to hide or drive out parts of ourselves that we are ashamed or afraid of. Unfortunately, any parts of ourselves that we do not face go undercover. Parts of ourselves that we are ashamed of go into hiding and operate beneath our awareness, hidden in our shadows. We may think that we are preventing them from acting out by ignoring them and trying not to give them life, but in reality, we are just blind to how they are acting out.

The stretch for our Heart King is to see all that is in our psyche, in our Kingdom, even our awful and evil. This is the only way we can truly know ourselves, the only way to have any choice as to who we are.

When we disown our Predator, who stepped up in the first place to try and protect us, we try to push it out of sight into our shadows. We turn against this part of ourselves, and as a result, it turns against us. All aspects of ourselves that we reject, hate, and fear, reject and hate and fear us back. In our ignored and suppressed inner darkness, our Predator corrodes and becomes the part of us that hates and predates on the world. It also becomes our Inner Critic who cruelly predates on and endlessly shames us. Our Inner Critic's targets anywhere we struggle; our Crumbling King, our Frozen Lover, any part of us that is wounded.

Our Predator holds primal natural power, and no matter how we try, we cannot keep a lid on potency such as this. Maybe we can usually keep it in check, but then we get drunk or become extremely tired, and it slips past our conscious control, and we do or say something horrible. We protest our innocence, saying, "it wasn't me", "I'm not like that", or "I don't know where that came from. It must have been the drink talking". Even while we claim innocence, we suffer from the shame of what we have done and endure a blizzard of self-criticism from our inner critic.

The Predator in Nature

Imagine a lion pack hunting to feed their young. Each lion is wild, healthy, capable, brave, strong and smart. The pack shows no malice when it hunts and kills. Each hunter is merely following its instincts to feed itself and its young. This stalking and hunting is not evil, abusive or shaming. It is just natural and contributes to the survival of all in the pack. In the wild, predation happens and keeps the ecological world in balance.

Predator and prey, the circuit of life and death, is the natural way of the world. As hunter-gatherers for 200,000 years, we were hunters and hunted. We are intimate with this cycle, and its primal energy exists in us; however, it is not likely to become particularly pronounced unless we need it. If we have a safe, affirming childhood, this predator energy will not get especially fired up.

If our childhood was unsafe and we were abused and perpetrated upon, we may have needed a mighty force to protect us in any way possible or impossible. This intensity, this possibility of inner power, is held by our Predator, that part of us that will never give in, will always look for an escape, will live off the desire for revenge, will never lie down and die. If we have been predated on in some way, or if we were just not safe as a child, or a teenager, this part of us will step up to try and keep us safe, or if not safe, to keep us alive. When we suffer from powerlessness, the most potent part that we have inside us steps forward to shield us from danger.

Many people get confused between Predator and Warrior. Warrior is strong, direct, and angry. Our Warrior sets our boundary and protects it. He steams in, even in the face of danger and threat. He draws his sword and holds his border, and if it is crossed, he fights with all he has. He doesn't hide his actions or his anger. This open strength is incredibly useful in life, but when we are children facing cruelty from adults who are far stronger than us, this open, straightforward Warrior is of little use. As a boy, our steadfast, courageous Warrior can be severely punished for opposing our abuser.

In contrast to our Warrior, our Predator uses his cunning mind as well as his unruly savage strength and is not emotionally fired. Our Predator is more likely to be emotionally cold and detached, able to plan his way through the situation without feelings. He doesn't stand in front of his enemy and openly oppose him or her. Like a leopard, he drops onto the back of his prey before that prey has even become aware that it is being stalked. He is focused, cunning and clever. He even enjoys the hunt and the blood of the kill.

If we are predated on in our childhood, our Warrior will be angry and want to fight back. However, because he is small and powerless, and because it is too dangerous to defy the one who is damaging him, he will not be able to take offensive action. Our intelligent Predator, however, will not feel so powerless and will make plans to evade, strike back, and eventually gain the advantage. He will form strategies to stay safe and get through, trying out different behaviours, evasions, and masks to see what works best.

As adults, the difficulty we have is that this predatory energy is not acknowledged or accepted in our culture. Because of this, we hide and disown this energy inside ourselves. Understandably, our Predator hates to be disowned, so he turns against us, as well as the world.

Those of us who have been in danger in our childhood know the instincts of the Predator. We also know that these instincts are not acceptable, so we try to hide them. Like any part of ourselves that we try to hide, repress, or deny, it still shows up, but now in unacknowledged patterns of human Predator and their human prey. We have this dark power in the first place because we were "bitten" in our past, and unless we face it and control it, we end up "biting" others, passing this vampire pain along. Having been 'bitten' by sexual abuse, rage or violence, we are in danger of becoming the one who delivers this to the following generation. It is excruciating to acknowledge that we are likely to hurt others in the same awful ways we were hurt. It is so terrible to know that, even though it is the last thing we want in the world, knowing how much it hurt and wounded us, we are likely to harm others in the very same way.

The good news is it doesn't have to be this way. If you have the courage to face your darkness within, you have a chance of knowing and working with this energy, or at least stopping it acting out. On our Retreats your Heart King will have a chance to work with your original wounding that bought this behaviour to life, and will enter a boundaried relationship with his Predator and Self Critic. This is a wild and deep process, and cannot be done here.

It is a brave move to look at your dark Predator and your inner predator, your Self Critic, to acknowledge that you are this. When you do this, you own up to yourself and your inner darkness, and you bring your Predator to the light of your King's conscious awareness.

This is the step you have the opportunity to undertake now.

Wounded Behaviour of the Predator Archetype

- I am a pathological **liar and manipulator**.
- My behaviours are associated with the sociopath, psychopath, and antisocial personality disorder.
- I will make up and say anything to achieve my aims.
- I repeat lies incessantly while ignoring and dismissing concrete evidence.
- I distort, practice deception, break promises, and blame my victim.
- I tell small, large, and malicious lies to feel better.
- I lie boldly, brashly and to your face.
- I don't care if you don't believe what I say.
- I state that everyone else is a liar.
- I believe that anyone who disagrees with me is either jealous or attacking me.
- I ignore the rights and feelings of others.
- I treat others harshly or with **callous** indifference.
- I don't feel guilt or remorse for my behaviour.
- I am cold and lacking in empathy.
- I will trespass on others with little reflection or moral conflict.
- I'm nakedly ambitious, ruthless, and aggressive.
- I antagonise and manipulate others.
- I encourage social intolerance and the acceptance of violence.
- I am sexist, a bigot, **racist**, narcissistic, misogynist, and a bully.
- I use these labels as excuses to hurt, humiliate, and degrade others.
- I demonise others. I'm happy to shock and offend. I aim to gain notoriety.
- I degrade, stigmatise and marginalise others.

- My actions don't match my words.
- I leave the other continually trying to work out the meaning behind my behaviours.
- My motives seem to be at cross-purposes.
- I sow **confusion** to pull my victims more profoundly into my web.
- I will be loving, appreciative, and understanding, and then out of the blue, I will return to punishing and abusing.
- I can appear **outwardly** functional and successful.
- I entice at first with great charisma and calculated charm.
- My true nature will reveal itself over time, especially when an important milestone has been passed or a relationship or agreement has been made.
- In relationships, I deceive, manipulate and abuse without remorse.
- I will isolate my partner from friends, family, and anyone who can help them or who presents a different view to me.
- Once I have isolated my partner from all competing relationships, I abandon all restraint and attack and abuse at will.
- **Over time** I make systematic attacks on anything you love or believe in, within and outside of you.
- I attack and start arguments with your family and parents. I belittle and bully your children and drive off your friends.
- I pour scorn on your achievements and laugh at your passions and hopes.
- I try to destroy anything that gives you worth.
- I want you to feel worthless, powerless, and useless.
- I want you without hope, dignity, strength, or self-confidence.
- I love watching you become unstable, start to lose it, and fall apart.
- My long-term aim is to isolate you completely.
- I make public accusations about you to bring public doubt about you.
- I try to disgrace you publicly. I want people to think badly of you and be on my side.
- I will use social occasions to put you down, force you to be quiet, make you look a fool, embarrass and shame you.
- I want to tarnish your image and destroy your reputation and career.
- I want to show that you are not capable of making reasoned decisions so that you know that no one believes you.
- I will **project** all of myself out onto you.
- I will continuously harass and put you down for being cruel, bullying, lying, etc., while completely denying that I am doing any of this himself.
- I tell you that you are wrong, not me and that you are evil and can't see it.
- When you get angry, I will tell you that you are the one full of unreasonable anger, not me. You're the crazy one. You are acting crazy.
- I will talk to others about you, then bring their view of how you are crazy to back up my own.

- I use fake friends to back me up that you are the villain, the bad one.
- **I enjoy hurting**, overpowering, and abusing others.
- I feel like I am winning when others are suffering.
- I don't learn any lessons from the consequences of my actions. I become a repeat offender.
- I leave my victim wounded and traumatised by my lack of feeling and decency.
- I suck all life and energy out of others, so they constantly feel **exhausted**.
- I let others know that they are not safe, that they are under threat.
- I make sure others have to watch out for my hurtful comments, my sly public digs, and my coded threats.
- I throw out little hints of love, of kindness, only to unpredictably cruelly smash things apart again.
- At times I will pretend to be the one to comfort and guide, the one to turn to, even though I have created your destruction.
- I will try to replace your reality with mine.
- I am happy **to break the rules** for my advantage and lack morality.
- I believe might is right, and rules are there to be broken.
- I consider ethical considerations a weakness, although I may practice a fake morality or pretend fairness.
- I am unethical and abusive towards my employees.
- I manoeuvre myself into **positions of power** and influence.
- I bully employees to lower their self-worth, independence, and self-esteem.
- As a narcissist I believe I am superior to all other people.
- I want to be better than others so I can exploit and mistreat them with contempt.
- I use power immorally for personal gain regardless of the damage and suffering I cause.
- I undermine relationships by gossiping, spreading rumours, leaching off and manipulating others to get them to do my bidding.
- I threaten to harm myself if you don't do as I want.
- I seek weakness, press buttons, and trigger reactions.
- **I gaslight** and bully psychologically.
- I try to control others with manipulation by making them feel like they are going mad and questioning the truth.
- I get my victims to question their reality, judgement, and mind, so they don't know what is real anymore. I deny what happened and tell you it never happened.
- I will never take responsibility for what I've done and will never be accountable.
- I am so subtle, slow and methodical that my victims are deeply damaged before they know they are targets.
- I put you down, letting you know that you can't do anything right and that you are worthless and bad.

- I want you to doubt yourself, question yourself, and be afraid for your own sanity.
- I present others as undesirable, detestable, and inadequate.
- I am deeply cordial, respectful, and blessing towards some, but cruel and inhumane to others. I make the other out to be lesser, bad, evil, and wrong. I split society into good and bad to contribute to intolerance and discrimination.
- I blame the victim. I corrupt the truth; I exaggerate or understate. I keep the focus off of the real issue.
- I assure my victims that the gas-lighting will not happen again, but it always does. I keep the ground unstable and shaky.

When confronted with my Predatorial behaviour I:
- I will deny it when I am caught lying. If I am confronted with proof, I will try to destroy and undermine the evidence. I show no remorse.
- I may become even more aggressive, hostile and challenging
- I deny responsibility. I make promises, then deny I have done so.
- I blame, accuse others and cast myself as the victim.
- I put up a front of arrogance and conceit.
- I claim I was set up, blamed, scapegoated, betrayed, singled out, and persecuted. I keep score of how others are responsible for my misery.
- I make sure I get revenge for all slights and deliver this revenge in an underhand sneaky fashion.

Bless you for having the courage to look into this part of yourself.

The Self Critic Speaks

Each paragraph is the voice of a different man

"You needy little shit. You are small and needy. You want to be seen all the time, but you are nothing. You don't know anything. You can be made tiny, so I can hold you in one hand and crush you. I can manipulate and control you.
I'm the one in control."

"I'm in control. I am constantly looking out for reasons for him not to be loved.
Reasons to show how he is not good enough. I barrage him. Even though he tries to hide from me, has even put up sheet steel to hold me back, I seep through."

"Fucking boohoo. Fuck you. Shut up. You're fucking worthless. You're fucking pathetic. You're fucking disgusting. I'm doing this for your own good. Stop putting women on a pedestal. You're a fucking worm. You are fucking inauthentic. You are full of pretence.
If I don't do this, you'll get fucked, betrayed, abandoned, it's happened before.
It will happen again if you give up your power to women."

"I don't want to hear you. Be quiet. Shut up. You're dirt. You're worthless. Nobody wants to hear you. Nobody is interested in what you say. It's shit anyway."

"Nothing you do will ever be good enough. Whatever you try, whatever you do.
Whoever you prove it to. I will show you, you are shit and will never be good enough.
You won't know where this has come from. You will think it is from your King or your Soul."

"I'm ever-present. Sometimes I'm silent, and he thinks I'm not there. But I'm just pretending.
I don't like him. Sometimes I wake him up at night. I'm very clever and convincing.
I look for patterns, evidence, confirmation.
I am the ruler.
I am in charge."

"You don't deserve this. Why did you step into this? What do you think you are doing?
I annihilate all your goodness. I am dark, violent, oppressive, cruel. A dementor.
I am the blackness sucking out all the gold."

"You never get this stuff right. You fucking shit-head. Round and round you go.
You will never ever get off. It will always be the same. You are never going to fix this.
I feel smug, powerful. I know this. I know what's going on. If you think you are going to get out of this, you never are. You'll never get out of this."

"I'm ever-present. Sometimes I'm silent, and he thinks I'm not there. But I'm just pretending.
I don't like him. Sometimes I wake him up at night. I'm very clever and convincing.
I look for patterns, evidence, confirmation. I am the ruler. I am in charge."

The Predator Speaks

Each paragraph is the voice of a different man. <u>Trigger Warning: this is violent and dark.</u>

"I am animal, automatic, instinctual. I want to hunt down and kill, especially when I feel vulnerable, unsafe, or not comfortable. I am animal. I hunt and kill."

"Fuck you. I will remove you from my world. If you challenge any part of my world, I will fuck you up. I will undermine you. I will remove you while making it look like you were the one in the wrong."

"I want to fucking kill. I love the hunt more than the fuck. I don't take no for an answer. Your no teases me even more. I just want to fuck you."

"You fucking cunt. I fucking destroy you. I take no prisoners. You've got no right to be here. You are dirt, and I will fuck you up. I don't give a fuck if you're bigger. There could be 3 of you, and I'll destroy you all. I'm a tank smasher. I'll rip you apart. You piece of dirt. You're so dirty I won't even touch you."

"I'm not dependent on you. I'm free. I'm powerful. You are only here to pleasure me.
You are only here to serve me. That's the only tiny part of my world I let you be in.
I want to fucking destroy you. I can humiliate you. I'm a god to you. I fucking own you.
I want to fuck you all day and every day. To fuck and destroy you. You're nothing.
I don't feel grief. I am perfect. I don't need a father.
I never, ever, ever, ever, ever, ever, ever, ever, ever am weak. I've never ever been weak.
No one can touch me. I am untouchable. I'm god to you, and you, with your tiny grief and pain. I am power. I am power. That's all I care about.
I could never let my weakness be seen by the world, so I became power.
I know how to manipulate power structures, how to move through power.
I need to be powerful so I never feel pain."

"I'm invincible. I can't be hurt. I'm totally uncaring. Detached, totally disconnected, no emotion. I am secret, manipulating. I take you by surprise. I get up when everyone else stays down. I take the extra step when you give up."

"I am a freak, deformed, one of a kind, abnormal, different. I like fucking people up, mixing up what they think. I am cruel. I don't give a fuck. I am the fucking SAS. I am the stormtrooper."

"I am a fucking black knight with an enormous sword. I will take your head off and hold it by the hair. I will burn the village down. I have zero compassion. Fuck you.
Fuck you for bringing your grief to me. I have true power, black power. This is preferable to loving power. I am high-octane fuel. I am remorseless. I suck energy. I am fast burning.
I burn from both ends."

"I want movement, action, sex, women, business, strength. I have to fuck, to fight, to tear things up. I want to fuck and take vengeance on the feminine, on the weak.
I want to take down idiotic men, to violate them, to scare the shit out of them.
I want utter wildness, deep in nature, with no one around. I want challenging, testing, no fear. I am raw earth universal skin shredding, howling, blood pouring, spunk filling rage energy, roaring with the beasts of the wild.
I am the conscious animal who knows his killer instinct inside out. I am the destructive abuser.
I can destroy children, young people, women, molest, kill, sometimes I want to do these

things. I do want to kill people, there are some people I would kill.
I want to kill my family, I wish I could just wipe them all out. I want to kill my mother, all the mothers, the whole fucking feminine line, fucking disgrace, fucking disgrace,
I want peace, justice, cleanliness of earth and in my blood."

Part 4

The Warrior Archetype

Introduction to Your Warrior

*"I am no bird; no net ensnares me:
I am a free human being with an independent will."*
Charlotte Bronte

The next step for your Healthy King is to know and come into a relationship with your Warrior.

Your Healthy Warrior is the doing, action-orientated part of yourself. Without a capable Warrior, nothing much will get done in your world.

Your active Warrior has a vital part to play in creating success in your world. When your King has a vision of what you want to achieve in your world, he gets your Magician to plan how to bring his dream into reality. Once your King is certain of his Magician's plan, he then turns to your Warrior and tasks your Warrior to do the work necessary to achieve his vision.

Your Warrior is the part of you that does the hard work to bring your King's projects to fruition. Without an effective Warrior, your Kingly vision is just a dream. Your Warrior is needed to bring your King's vision into reality. If your Warrior does not want to work or can't get out of bed, nothing happens.

*"Work is man's greatest function.
He is nothing, he can do nothing, achieve nothing without working."*
J M Cowan

In the past, the Warrior archetype was often a soldier. These days not many men work as soldiers, and for most, the Warrior is our worker. Your Warrior gets you to work day after day and seeks to build your profitable, successful career.

Much of your self-esteem depends on your Warrior. Your Warrior seeks to engage with the world and come out victorious. Each time your Warrior accomplishes a successful action, he builds your self-identity as competent and capable. He builds strength and self-definition through his effort and his struggle.

Your King and your Warrior both hold your self-esteem, but in different ways. Your King looks to your whole life and compares the success of your life against your vision for yourself. Your Warrior's self-esteem is on the line with every individual action and effort you make. Each time you step forward to try and achieve, you test your Warrior self. If you achieve your aim, you raise your self-esteem. Every individual success increases your Warrior belief that you are successful and capable.

> *"Step by step is the law of growth.*
> *God does not expect the Acorn to be a mighty oak*
> *before it has been a sapling."*
> George Carpenter

Your Warrior has many other ways of making an effort that contributes to the success of your world. You dig your garden, play sport, cultivate your robust and healthy body, and exercise. All your efforts go towards building a picture of yourself as capable and effective. As you thrive, you foster and strengthen your self-esteem.

With your healthy, growing, cultivated self-esteem, your Warrior builds your ego. Many traditions see ego as a disruptive force that you need to get over and put away. To say you should not have an ego hamstrings your Warrior. Your Warrior's ego is the platform you stand on as you engage with the world, particularly the working world. Without your ego, you have no firm foundation. Saying your Warrior builds your ego doesn't mean that you need to engage with the world solely from your ego Warrior. Ideally, you will engage with the world from your Heart King, who loves and directs your potent, powerful Warrior. You are not looking to 'get over your ego' but rather to have your King direct your Healthy Warrior ego.

> *"When you love who you are,*
> *there is no thing unconquerable,*
> *no thing unreachable."*
> Ramtha

A strong Warrior without a Healthy King directing him can be damaging to the world, as we have seen since the beginning of time. All good Warriors love and need a strong King leading them. Your Warrior holds your anger, and without the discriminating, love-oriented discernment of your King, your assertive anger can be easily overused and have a destructive effect.

In this section on the Warrior, your Heart King will get to know your Healthy Warrior and your two wounded Warriors. These are your Too Much Warrior (called your Bully) and your Too Little Warrior (called your Pushover).

If you are in Too Much Warrior, it is likely that you work too hard and too aggressively. If you are in Too Little Warrior, you struggle to get anything done and do not build successfully. Both can harm your world.

Once you know where you are, either in Too Much or Too Little Warrior, you can notice when you behave this way.

> *"It takes courage to grow up and turn out to be who you really are."*
> E E Cummings

Behaviours of the Healthy Warrior Archetype

- I am an **individual**. I stand alone or solidly together, but I am always authentically myself.
- I establish my strong sense of self, my **ego**; I assert my personal identity and my belief in who I am. I hold myself and build my power. I am self-affirming.
- Each time I succeed in what I do, I confirm my individuality and let myself know that this self I am building is the right self.

> "It is a psychological fact that
> man always conforms to the image he holds of himself.
> Change that image, and you change his actions, his reactions,
> his environment, his world."
> Jack Holland

- I am self-confident and ruggedly assertive.
- I have a right to be alive. I doggedly defend myself and ferociously fight for my survival.
- I am grounded and realistic. I know the best action to take in each moment. I am aware of my strengths and my weakness.
- I am surrendered to and obediently serve my King.
- I **carry out the mission** of my King. I am prepared to leave the comfortable and ordinary behind to achieve his extraordinary mission. I follow my King's higher calling.
- I make his mission achievable and concrete in the world. Without my efforts, it is just an idea. Without me, it will not be birthed into reality. I always do my honourable best.
- I am **principled**. I try to stick to what I believe is right and what is wrong. I am dependably consistent with my ideals.
- I have strong personal convictions and constant morals. I can be relied on to be fair and truthful.
- I am honest and thrifty. I have a high moral character. I have integrity. I am trustworthy. I am humane, humble and honourable.
- I have discovered my limits, so I am realistic about my limitations.
- I follow should, must, and ought to. I follow simple rational logic and concrete objective truth.
- I stand for the truth. I give hope and reliable protection.

> "A hero is one who heals his own wounds
> And then shows others how to do the same."
> Yung Pueblo

- I hold to the **values** of duty, honour, loyalty, and sacrifice. I am not self-serving, and I care enough for others to die for them.
- I am conscientious and ethical. I try to maintain high standards, especially in my work. I am orderly, honest, and do the right thing.
- I am emotionally honest. I own my feelings. I look carefully to know my motivations. I do not deny what is going on inside, and I do not whitewash myself. I see myself "warts and all", and I let you know this side of me too.
- I restrain my instinctive drives. I won't give in to them or express them too freely. I won't let them drive me. I am naturally self-controlled.
- I keep a lid on my desires. Although it looks like I am not feeling much, I feel intensely. I just do not let it show much.
- I am **enthusiastic and daringly heroic**. I have a great passion for life.
- I am energetic, adventurous, progressive, striving, charismatic and exciting.
- I am virile and vital. I bring the power of life with me. I inspire excellence and success. I face forward, and I move towards.
- I am alert and awake. I do not sleep my way through life.

> "We are the heroes of our own story."
> Mary McCarthy

- I have **common sense**. I am grounded and objective. I am happy to make decisions and know that my choices will not please everyone.
- If it's not in my experience, it's not in my truth. I have integrity and am authentic.
- While I try to avoid making mistakes, I know that I won't always get it right. I learn from my mistakes and try not to make the same mistake twice. I am willing to acknowledge when I have messed up.
- I prefer a strong, narrow, single focus. I want to commit or not do it at all.
- I am a **loyal, trustworthy friend**. I am affectionate and lovable.
- Once I trust, I form strong cooperative alliances and friendships. I treat friends as equals.
- I am very dedicated to groups and resourceful movements. I build a purposeful community.
- I will sacrifice my interests for the good of the group or a friend. I advance co-operation and stability.
- I consistently support my friends and family. I fiercely protect those I love. I provide vital, safe, sensitive help to those suffering and in crisis.

> "Never underestimate the power of
> a loosely knit group working for a good cause ...
> their power is beyond their numbers."
> Peace Pilgrim

- I idealise **leaders**. I want good authentic leadership. I want my leader to be just, virtuous and effective. I want them to direct me so I can bring these qualities to my action-orientated efforts.
- I serve leaders dutifully, loyally and courageously. I love to be capably in service to the greater good.
- I carry out my Sovereign's inspiring mission, protect the gentle Lover, make real, and define the kingdom the Magician understands, imagines and plans for.
- I leave the **old behind**, encourage transformation, determine a new course, step out of the familiar, and confront uncertainty.
- I frequently explore the unknown, take risks, make mistakes, and overcome obstacles.
- I know that, at times some things need destroying so that something new and better can be birthed.
- I overcome my unconscious habits. I separate from my parents and my culture to define myself and unfold and inhabit my unique destiny.
- I won't be tied up by social conventions. I will do the right thing, even if I am shamed and condemned for doing it. I do not let others' opinions of me stop me.
- I recognise my mortality and know that life is fragile. This doesn't depress me. It fuels my actions.
- I don't hesitate. I know every determined act counts, and I act as if each is my last.

> "Action is the single most effective antidote to depression, anxiety, stress, fear, wrong, guilt and of course, immobility.
> It is virtually impossible to be depressed and active at the same time."
> Wayne Dyer

Skills:

- I am a **natural catalysing leader** of groups. I am good at making alliances and maintaining the stability and longevity of a group.
- As a leader, I have a solid, stable, undemonstrative, and commanding presence.
- I relate through shared constructive activity and action empathy.
- I use jokes and humour to connect with others and reduce stress.
- I take the initiative. I love a challenge, and I love to provide challenges for others.
- I make things happen. I can be relied on to push into what is next, to do the next best thing.

- I am honourable, and people trust me to lead the way forward and find a way to provide. They trust me to look after their best interests, be fair, and not have favourites. I carry others forward with my strength.
- I am a supportive **mentor**. I am invested in empowering others. I am not threatened by others gaining power, insight, and capability.
- I help others save face and minimise humiliation. I always praise the achievements of subordinates.

> "Warriors are not what you think of as warriors.
> The Warrior is not someone who fights...
> The Warrior is one who sacrifices himself for the good of others.
> His task is to take care of the elderly, the defenceless,
> those who cannot provide for themselves,
> and above all, the children, the future of humanity."
> Sitting Bull

- I **provide and accomplish**. I have admirable **ability**.
- Through deliberate effort, I am capable of achieving my purpose. I have a "can-do" attitude.
- I manifest naturally. I bring skill, strength, and determination to every endeavour.
- I bring enriching resources into the kingdom. I am hardworking, responsible, and reliable. I ensure self-sufficiency. Through my work, I bring financial security.
- I take risks when necessary to keep us abundant.
- I choose, acquire, own, and build. I love to see evidence of my efforts and my success.
- I focus my mind and body by being continually aware and attentive.
- I train to upgrade my skills, strength, self-discipline and focus and maintain mastery.

> "If people knew how hard I work to get my mastery,
> it would not seem so marvellous after all."
> Michelangelo

- I maintain clean, clear, gentle, and firm **boundaries.** I hold my ultimate boundary, my ego-self, which forms a boundary between what is "me" and what is "not me".
- Within my boundary, I stand for security, stability, and order. I make agreements and fulfil them, creating trust. I am safe to be around.
- I reduce dissipating disorder and destructive chaos. I stand firm so others can rally around me.

- **I protect.** I am protective. I defend myself and those who need my protection. I love and care for the little boy inside me.
- I keep the balance. I ensure inclusive safety. I protect the weak and the vulnerable.
- I destroy self-serving tyrants. I liberate the humiliated, enslaved and oppressed.
- I will not allow myself or others to be controlled. I won't let tyrants have power over us. I will not be conquered.
- I use my solid strength to improve life for all of us.
- I am regenerative. I bring help and hope to many.
- I **serve** the world, the common good, and the larger purpose. I am committed and faithful. I know the importance of a team effort, so I make alliances with other noble warriors. I want to be on a team with elite warriors.
- I am dutiful, conscientious, calm, and patient. My commitment is to something greater than myself.
- I want to serve and improve the world. I intend to make a difference and do something extraordinary. I am important in the world.
- I will leave the safe and the comfortable if I feel a calling, even at a high cost to myself.

> "It is only through labour and painful effort,
> by grim energy and resolute courage,
> that we move on to better things."
> Theodore Roosevelt.

Gifts:

- I appropriately gain and steward **personal power**. I know that if I am not dangerous, I have no power. If I pull out my sword, I intend to use it. I am generous, humane, wise and merciful in my use of force.
- I have power over myself, self-discipline, self-restraint, and strong willpower. I have strength and ability and take responsibility for building myself, defining myself, and building my autonomy and self-esteem.
- I take personal responsibility. I accept that I am the cause of my life and the source of my power. I am responsible for what happens here.
- I trust my compassionate truth, and I act on it with absolute conviction.
- I maintain my independence. I will not be indebted.
- I am self-reliant and in control of my life and destiny.
- I steward and appropriately use my **healthy anger**.
- Using my anger, I burn off what is old, decayed and outdated in me. I renew myself so that I am ready for what is coming next.
- I use my anger to stay steadily strong. My anger gives me the energy to push through, to complete when I am exhausted.

- When necessary, I exert controlled aggression and destruction meaningfully.

> *"Anybody can become angry — that is easy,*
> *but to be angry with the right person and to the right degree*
> *and at the right time and for the right purpose, and in the right way*
> *— that is not within everybody's power and is not easy."*
> Aristotle

- I bring **successful practical action** to my world.
- I don't intend to lose. I push, separate, and differentiate.
- I am well organised and self-controlled. I take the initiative and make things happen.
- I am resourceful, inspiring, and hardworking. I maintain high standards. I love meaningful work.
- I follow my strong instinctive **drive.**
- I have the courage, persistence, willpower, endurance, and stamina required for achievement. I assert myself upon the world, and I affect the world around me.
- I bring change, affect evolution and make my mark on the world. I energise and motivate by example.
- I am courageous, adventurous and audacious and can achieve great things with risk-taking and daring.
- I am capable of coping with intense stress and **high-pressure** situations.
- I hold the virtue of **courage**. I take the best action in each moment.
- I am noble, inspiring and heroic.
- I love to drive forward. I take the offensive and am ready to face the challenges in front of me.
- I prove my strength, and I resist my weaknesses. I am strong. If I am not strong, I find out how to be strong.

> *"Courage and perseverance have a magnetic talisman,*
> *before which difficulties disappear and obstacles vanish."*
> John Quincy Adams

- I have tremendous willpower, fortitude, and determination.
- I withstand pain and suffering and move beyond it. I can tolerate a great deal of physical damage or punishment. I don't complain.
- I overcome adversity and am resilient. I focus on uncomfortable and unpleasant tasks. I can endure suffering with quiet strength. I can face darkness and not be overwhelmed.

- I am willing to make personal sacrifices to achieve for myself and others. With my courage, I will put myself in danger for others. My example encourages others to be strong and confident.
- I can transform all difficulties into something valuable.

> *"Adversity is the midwife of genius."*
> Napoleon Bonaparte

- I am a **reformer** and an activist. I step up to improve the world and make it a better place.
- I am idealistic. I am always working to improve things. I advocate for change. I crusade for what is right. I instinctively know just how good things could be.
- I strive to make a difference. I want to be useful. I stand up for justice and equality.

The Warrior Speaks

Each paragraph is the voice of a different man.

"I am boundaried. I know when I am right. I feel it in my gut. I show up. I make sure everything is in place. I work towards the bigger picture. I keep things running smoothly."

"I have endurance. I stick at it through darkness and cold. I enjoy getting over obstacles. Once I'm engaged, I don't look back. I make sure the mission is completed. Once I draw a line in the sand, I am immovable."

"I am community minded. I serve my community. I want happiness for all, not just for myself. I am of service. I have common sense. My family relies on me."

"I believe in being fair. I am in service to my King. I get the job done. I work well with others. I am open to others' input."

"I have strength. I take action when I see things that need doing. I am very stable. I know I can keep going. I have deep faith in my ability. I have a powerful bullshit detector. I cut down to the essence of something."

"I believe in growth. Maintenance is not enough. Change requires effort. I am good at being really clear. I enjoy strength and skill."

"I want success for us all. I do my best. I do my best. My best is good enough, and I wish for more. I value boundaries. I have passion. I know my Too Little and Too Much is damaging. I balance myself."

"I'm self-confident. I am assertive. I deliver. I wait for orders from my King. I am very loyal. I am clean action in the world. I am cleanly powerful. I take direct action. I find a way through. I do it in a good way."

"I delight in seeing my King. I rely on him. I take on challenges. No matter how difficult. That is who I am. I revel in exercise. I love being outdoors. I love being part of something powerful. I recognize the team can do more than I can do alone."

"I am responsible for cleaning up the messes of my shadow. I hold my identity of who I am and what I can do. I build a kingdom my King can be proud of. I look for his blessing for what I achieve. I integrate and connect. I have incredible strength and power."

"I work hard. I have established myself. I look after my children. I have accumulated assets. I am sensible. I know my limits and when I am getting past them. I do my best and make the best of it. I won't work in an unhealthy environment. I keep my bullying, overinflated warrior in check. I rarely get in fights anymore. My bullying has become playful."

"I need my King to give me the bigger picture. I need his direction to know where I'm going, what I'm doing. I look after my body. I go to the gym. I created my strong body for now and for the future. I restrict my drinking. I eat properly. I have self-discipline."

"I am a get-up and get-it-done guy. I get stuff done. I am respected and listened to. My anger shows itself as strength. My boundaries are clear. Others know where they stand. I step up in a clean way to handle conflict. I communicate clearly. I can say no and hold to it."

"I protect those in need. I protect those weaker than me. I support others. I am a powerful presence others can rely on and feel safe within. I keep the kingdom safe."

"I am the one who gets our life made. I build my career. I am a powerhouse. I step up. I step forward. I don't avoid. I create a stable and healthy environment. I make the King's vision real. I am able and level-headed. I will not be held back by fear.
I am proud to be in service."

The Bully Archetype
Too Much Warrior

'The lives of men, so fragile, so deadly.
Left alone, they lit and warmed.
Let run rampant, they would destroy the very things
they were meant to illuminate.
Embryonic bonfires, each bearing a seed of destruction so potent
it could tumble cities and dash kings to their knees."
Brandon Sanderson

In the previous chapter, your King got to know his Healthy Warrior. As we saw earlier with your King, your Warrior also comes in three forms: Healthy, Too Much, and Too Little. Here you will get to know your Too Much Warrior, your Bully.

This character is hard to be around. He is harsh, brutal and intrusive. He is hard to reason with. He is damaging and hurtful.

As always Heart King, as you get to know him here, and inside yourself, try and suspend your judgements, and try to keep your heart open to this part of yourself.

Welcome to the Bully.

We will start by looking at our Playful Boy to see how he was wounded.

In an ideal childhood, your Warrior Boy would have been held in a "good enough way" so that he could have experimented with himself and developed a healthy, positive sense of his identity. Few boys, however, have this opportunity, and most, if not all, boys are wounded to some extent in their adventurous, playful childhood. Because of this, when he grows up into an adult, he is likely to have Healthy Warrior qualities and other less healthy behaviours that come from his reaction to being wounded as a child.

How a Warrior Boy is Wounded

Your Warrior Boy had essential core needs that needed to be satisfied for him to grow up with a healthy sense of self.

These included:
- Having space to experiment with himself.
- Regular approval and encouragement.
- Being allowed to make mistakes, fail and try again without being shamed.
- Being provided with appropriate adventures to test himself.
- Having opportunities and support to form his solid sense of self.

Sadly, your Boy may not have been held in a loving, permissive way and may have lived in a harsher, more punishing world. If this was true for you, you might have been subject to some of the wounding actions seen below.

Wounding family actions and events:
- Facing physical abuse, not being protected, being threatened with harm or death.
- Being exposed to violence or being forced to watch cruel acts.
- Having his precious objects or pets threatened with destruction or destroyed.
- Being bullied, hurt, and scared. Being disciplined in a punitive and harsh manner. Being singled out for punishment, responded to unpredictably, and raged against.
- Being humiliated, belittled, name-called, yelled and sworn at. Being made the butt of demeaning jokes.
- Being approved of for bullying others and encouraged to be violent in sports.
- Being used and taken advantage of, having onerous duties imposed on him and having to undertake excessive chores.
- Having his confidence undermined, not being praised for his success, having no interest shown in him, not noticing significant events in his life, and not wanting to discuss or be interested in his daily life.
- Being overprotective and enmeshed with him, denying him opportunities to grow or take risks, treating him as a child when he is an adolescent.

Resulting Beliefs

In the face of this relentless damage to his Warrior self-esteem, the Boy may give up and accepts that he is less than, that he cannot be himself, and is not capable or successful. Otherwise, he may fight against these painful, wounding beliefs and try way too hard to prove them wrong.

In reality, he probably swings in a bipolar fashion between giving in to these beliefs and fighting against them.

Fighting Against his Beliefs:
- I am great because I dominate others. If I defeat others, then I prove that I exist.
- I am strong when I force myself on others. I show I have value when I am strong.
- I meet my desires by forcing others to comply with them.
- No one cares about me, so I don't care about others. I only care about myself.
- When I am forced to comply, I am passive-aggressive until I explode.

Fighting against undermining childhood beliefs, the wounded Warrior Boy grows into the adult Warrior with Too Much Warrior essence. I have named him the Bully. He seeks to hide his painful wounds and his lack of self-belief by proving to the world that he is the opposite of his beliefs.

Wounded Behaviour of the Bully Archetype

- I am the hyper-masculine **male:** hard, aggressive, unfeeling and invulnerable. I am a rugged individual.
- It's all up to me. I have to do it all. Without me, everything would fall apart.
- I am **absolute**. I am strong, or I am weak. I am a warrior or a victim.
- I will never be a victim. I hate weakness. I will never be weak.

> *"When you have a persistent sense of heartbreak and gutwrench,*
> *the physical sensations become intolerable,*
> *and we will do anything to make those feelings disappear. "*
> Bessel A. van der Kolk

- I am a **self-centred, self-interested individual**. I focus solely on myself.
- I bruisingly compete over everything.
- It's every man for himself and me against everyone else. Only the strongest survive, and I will do whatever it takes to win. If I don't grab it, someone else will. I get what I want. I put my needs first, even if I hurt, walk over or mistreat others.
- I rely on no one. I prove myself to be self-sufficient, independent, and autonomous.
- I don't care about public service or public interest.
- I am an aggressive capitalist. I work for my profit. I don't care who or what I damage in the process.
- I ruthlessly exploit the earth. The earth and all its resources are for me to seize.

> *"Lazy parasites, who perch on you just to satisfy their needs,*
> *they do not come to alleviate your burdens, hence, their mission is*
> *to distract, detract and extract, and make you live in abject poverty."*
> Michael Bassey Johnson

- I am opinionated, self-assured, arrogant and cocky, and I have a very **inflated view of myself**. I am egocentric.
- I am greedy, envious, and demanding. I rely on external achievements to bring me fulfilment.
- I am overwhelmingly greedy. I only give to receive. I never have enough. I want endless possessions and fear their loss. I hungrily gather all the glory for myself.
- I must always to be correct and have the last word. I am bluntly dogmatic and obstinately self-righteous.
- If it's not going my way, I will brutally destroy it all rather than let someone more capable take over. I can be vengeful, vicious and even murderous.

> "Good wins in the end because evil is a self-destructive,
> cannibalistic force that Inevitably
> engorges upon itself."
> Ken Poirot

- I am **invincible** and will always be victorious. I will beat you every time. Being the ruthless winner is at the core of all I do. I am obsessed with success.
- I am invulnerable and cannot be touched. I will not be indebted to you or anyone else.
- I am dominantly strong. No one is stronger than me.
- I dangerously over-extend myself and am not aware I am doing it. I am thoughtlessly and habitually reckless. I do not recognise my weaknesses.
- I don't understand why you find it hard to be around me. I resent being misunderstood. I feel hurt and rejected by you but never show it.
- My actions are brutishly overdone and brashly dramatic. I dominate to reassure myself that I am potent.

> "Anger is just anger. It isn't good. It isn't bad. It just is.
> What you do with it is what matters. It's like anything else.
> You can use it to build or to destroy.
> You just have to make the choice."
> Jim Butcher

- I am ragingly **angry**. I am moody and wrathfully turbulent.
- I am abusive, irritable and hot-tempered. I have threatening temper tantrums and violent outbursts. I am objectionably impatient.
- I do not experience any emotions except anger which is my default mode.
- I am in attack mode, aggressive, conquering, and endlessly combative.
- I am acutely sensitive to you disrespecting me. I get into arguments, disputes and fights.

> "Bullying builds character like nuclear waste creates superheroes.
> It's a rare occurrence and often does much more damage than endowment."
> Zack W. Van

- I am **dominating, bullying**, domineering, power-hungry, and controlling. I abusively overuse my will. I humiliate you to intimidate you.
- The power I exert is barren, brutal and callous. I am harsh, hard and loveless.
- I am all bluff and swagger. I am abrasively proud and boastfully overbearing. I suck up all the energy in the room.
- I do not recognise the difference between self-defence and attack. When I defend myself, I am aggressive and wounding.
- My brash might makes me right. There is no space for you. I am frighteningly threatening and may be violent.

- I want you deprived and dis-empowered. You must respect me, but I won't respect you. You are not my equal, and I don't treat you with respect.
- I dominate and control my environment, the people around me, what they do and how they do it.
- Do it my way. My way is the only way. There is no other possible way. If you don't do it my way, I attack you.

> "The harder a man feels compelled to be, the weaker his ego is."
> Chimamanda Ngozi Adichie

- I believe the world is **obnoxiously hostile** to me, so I retaliate. I insult, menace, hurt and punish.
- I stimulate anger and frustration in others, and when they react, they confirm my brutish beliefs.
- I bluster, argue and provoke. I accuse, betray and let down. I battle and persecute. I blame and complain. When people show that they are sick of me, they confirm my view of the world.
- I create **adversarial relationships**. I am confrontational, intimidating, belligerent and wounding.
- Every interaction is a test of will. I want to fight with you, to compete, to show you that I am the best.
- Do what I say, or there will be consequences. I work to keep you off-balance, suffocated, scared and insecure.
- I insultingly treat you unjustly, so you are afraid of me. I make sure you do not ally with others to oppose me. I turn others against you.

> "I am awfully greedy; I want everything from life.
> When I do not succeed, I get mad with anger."
> Simone de Beauvoir

- I am a territorial gangster, and I **fight everything**. I am dangerous.
- I'm into firepower, the joy of destruction. I don't care about human life. I love killing. I'm going to kill as many as I can, as fast as I can, and I'm going to enjoy it.
- I am a sadist and a bestial masochist. I love to hurt others cruelly.
- I am a barbarian berserker. I run amok. I am the death's head Nazi SS.
- I penetrate your boundaries, disregard your rights, and violate your integrity.
- I am a **high-conflict** personality. I create and escalate conflict.
- I do not accept the blame if I do something wrong. I cannot see things through others' eyes. I will not admit I contributed in any way to the situation.
- I will not take responsibility or apologise. I always have someone else to blame. I am the victim here.

- I am emotionally aggressive, and I lose control of my raging emotions. When my feelings overwhelm me, I behave in alarming and disturbing ways.
- My thinking is all or nothing. You are totally with me, or you are totally against me. If you are against me, I hate you.

> "People who love themselves, don't hurt other people.
> The more we hate ourselves, the more we want others to suffer."
> Dan Pearce

- I **punish** you when you get it wrong. I am very hard on you, punitive, shaming and unjust.
- Don't make mistakes, or I will penalise you. I attack your imperfections.
- I am inflexible. I am intolerant of outsiders or people I don't know. I am cruel to them and want to get rid of them.
- I am likely to be doing the very things that I hate others doing. My actions are full of contradictions. Do as I say, not as I do.
- I won't look within. I project all my failings onto you.
- If I am going to be defeated, I smash everything up rather than surrender.
- I hold resentments. I am vengeful and vindictive. I will get you back.

> "It's an evil fate to fall into the hands of a persecutor
> who was once persecuted."
> Bangambiki Habyarimana

- I am **callous**, cynical, and contemptuous of your feelings, rights, and suffering.
- I lack remorse and am indifferent to how I have hurt or stolen from you. I don't care about you. I don't feel guilty when I mistreat you.
- I learned how to be hard at a very young age. It was not okay for me to cry or show any weakness as a child. I learned early not to let anyone push me around. I relentlessly fought back. I dominated and defeated any softness in myself.
- I am offensively tough and expect you to be tough. I demand that you behave in typically hyper-masculine ways.
- I use people as commodities. I discard them when I have no further use for them.

> "Be always vigilant about eagles, crows and vultures around you.
> In a flash, they may pounce and pinch your peace,
> prosperity, joy and happiness,
> blur your vision with their filthy wings,
> vilify your fame with dirt and halt your progress."
> Lord Robin

- Don't talk to me about feelings. **Fuck feelings**. I am cold steel. All emotion is weakness. The only feeling I have is overbearing anger and the sadistic, erotic pleasure of hurting.

- I don't recognise gentler feelings and emotions. If I do notice them, I judge them as soft and weak.
- I am continually stonewalling. "I can take it", "you'll never get me". I am endlessly, numbly stubborn.
- I control my emotions. I despise your useless vulnerability, your pathetic fragility, and your disgusting weakness.
- There is no way I will be vulnerable. I stay **numb** and detached so I won't feel exposed or defective. I am shut down. I am a rock.
- I won't let you hurt me. I am strongly armoured against you. I protect my feelings and keep you at a safe emotional distance.
- I keep alone by working endlessly. My work keeps me from having to have emotional contact. Anger is the only emotion I feel when I am working.
- To love you would give you power over me, and I won't have that.
- In my love relationship, I don't get your frustration with my numbness and distance. Your calling for me to be close and present confuses and confounds me. I end up feeling misunderstood and so step even further away. Can't you see I am trying my best, that I am working hard to provide for us all? Isn't that enough for you?
- Beneath my blunt exterior, I feel hurt and rejected. I suck up my pain to show how tough I am.
- My deepest fear is that I will be rejected and humiliated. I am afraid I will be fired, divorced, criticised, or found wanting.
- I ignore the pain, sadness, and fear of my childhood. Though it haunts me, I turn away from it and try to forget it.

"The devil is always around the corner."
Will Leamon

- I **deny myself**, so my needs are not met. I am then resentful, angry and moody.
- I use excessive will to control my body, and I treat it like a machine. I do not acknowledge my limitations.
- I push myself through sheer will without thinking or feeling.
- I am reckless with my health and stamina, and I take them for granted. I overlook your health and well-being and treat you as I treat myself.
- I suffer stoically. I will not cry or ask for help. I avoid being needy or clingy at all costs.
- I am extraordinarily resilient. I can absorb any amount of physical punishment.
- I am a **workaholic.** I have driving ambition, so I won't stop working. I work harder. I work more. Work is my solution to everything.
- I take on too much responsibility.
- I try to "save" the world and give until I am completely depleted. I can only accept my true worth and right to belong by endlessly doing "good" deeds. I rescue the "victim" and build unhealthy co-dependency.
- I am endlessly busy and so full of accomplishments, engagements and activities that I am chronically tired and eventually burn out.

- I am burned out because I live life as a remorseless struggle. I compete against others, and I battle with the parts of myself I don't like. I see life as a desperate challenge, and I fight against it.
- I bring the war home. I am never out of an aggressive fight. I fight battle after battle. I grapple with the violent dragon inside myself.

> "The lives of men, so fragile, so deadly.
> Let run rampant, they would destroy the very things they were meant to illuminate.
> Embryonic bonfires, each bearing a seed of destruction so potent
> it could tumble cities and dash kings to their knees."
> Brandon Sanderson

- I am impulsive, don't plan, and have a reckless disregard for my own and others' safety. I hazardously overextend myself.
- I am **irresponsible** and exploitative in my sexual relationships. I don't value committed relationships. I don't care about building a home and am away from home a lot. I am quickly bored. I have harmful affairs. I dissolve relationships.
- I put myself and others at risk and in dangerous situations without considering the consequence.
- I am the **rebel**. I am locked in my traumatic adolescence. I mistrust and hate authority. I love the renegade underdog.
- You can't tell me what to do, and you cannot criticise me.
- If you thwart me, it is because you are the evil oppressor.
- I **won't conform to social norms**, and I don't have a problem with bending or breaking the law for my benefit. I will conn you for my advantage, pleasure or profit.
- I feel disdainful of ordinary ways of living. I am exempt from everyday life, and I look down on you for living conventionally. I don't have to fit in. I don't care what others think of me.
- I am the criminal, the outlaw, and the thief. I take pride in getting one over you. I don't let morals get in my way. I break the law if it benefits me. I steal and take without consent.
- I take advantage of the system. I am better than the law, and I abuse its weakness.

> "Why do we desire, above all other things,
> that which has the greatest power to destroy us?"
> Margaret Rogerson

The Bully Speaks

Each paragraph is the voice of a different man.

"I am Too Much Warrior. My drive is to charge at life. I go 200mph at everything. I win, I excel, I achieve to the max at everything. I am busy, much busier than I should be.
I am stress, high blood pressure. I don't pay attention to relationships. I take them for granted. I don't focus on them."

"It's your fault, not mine. I always make myself look best at the expense of making others look small. It's never my fault, never. I won't take advice."

"I'm relentless. As long as my body will go, I'll go. I feel a lot of anger. To step up, I close off all my other emotions. To be able to push through, I can't allow myself to feel.
I harden into survival mode. I shut out my grief and fear to get the job done."

"I have absolutely no tolerance. Just fuck off and let me do it. I will do it right and quicker. I know what needs to be done. You are fucking useless. A bunch of useless cunts. There is only one way of doing it. And it's my way."

"Get out of my way. I want to smash you up. You infect me. I don't breathe in around you. I might catch your insecurity. I won't even look at you. I choose hatred, bad feelings, being nasty."

"I feel fucking invincible. I need to smash some shit up. I need to be heard. I should be heard more. I've got some shit to say."

"Like me. Fucking like me. I want to take revenge on the world. A lot of people are scared of me. I'm fucking angry."

"People are stupid. People are such idiots. What a bunch of fucking idiots. I have to be the best. I am fiercely competitive. I sneer at other's mistakes. I hate people who are late.
If you get in my way I shame you, dismiss you, be angry with you. You are in my way. Don't you realise where I'm going is so much more important than you?
I hate it when someone rings me up to say hello. Do you think I'm just sitting around doing nothing? Just because you have nothing in your life. You have no appreciation of how busy I am."

"I am disdainful of the ordinary. I want danger, risk, adventure. No one understands me. I know my family want me at home. But I've got stuff to do. I am on a journey. It's my journey. It's important. I want to be seen doing it."

"I overreach. People get caught in my rage. When I'm triggered, I swing out. I am vicious in the way I communicate. I reach 11 out of 10 on the dial."

"I am a hothead. I come from rage, challenge. I'm ready to come out and be violent. I brought this shit out at school. I bullied kids for weakness, difference, newness. I shout, at work, at my son. I am designed to scare."

"I am fearless, unthinking, really, really uncaring. I get my way in every moment. I bully through fear and aggression. I hate being ignored. I lose my temper when I'm ignored, the red mist comes down. Everything is fair game. I smash things up. I rage at things."

"I am intolerant of people, animals, my children. I bully to get my way. I can be fucking scary. I can shout really loud. I create a powerful ripple, a shockwave. I relish my power."

"I am relentless. Eyes down, I step in, one after another. I never come up for air. However long it takes. I trudge on. Unaware of any consequences for myself or others."

"I drive forward. I walk over everything that needs walking over. I ignore niceties, feelings, convention. I make it happen.
I get fucked off with people not doing it good enough. I push them out the way so I can do it properly. I am hard, free of compassion. I just want to get it done. I am in your face. Brutal, justified."

The Pushover Archetype
Too Little Warrior

"It's not all bad.
"Heightened self-consciousness, apartness, an inability to join in,
physical shame and self-loathing—they are not all bad.
Those devils have been my angels."
Stephen Fry

As the Healthy King, you have become familiar with and established a relationship with your Bully, one side of your wounded Warrior. Now you have a chance to get to know your collapsed warrior who is deeply incapable.

Like your Bully, your Pushover suffered from a wounding childhood where your core needs were not met so that you could not develop a healthy sense of self.

Your core needs were the same as those listed for your Bully, and you were wounded by family actions just as your Bully was. Unlike your Bully, who fought against these wounding beliefs, you gave into them and so came to believe certain things about yourself.

Giving in to these Beliefs

- I have to let people take advantage of me, use, and control me.
- I have to let others hurt me. I must not be angry. I must not be aggressive or retaliate.
- I must put your needs and preferences above my own.
- I have no value. Anyone can walk over me.
- I am not important. Others will always have more than me.
- No one will protect me. They won't give me guidance or direction.
- I am weak.
- I can't take care of myself.
- I must be wholly enmeshed with an important other to survive or be happy. I don't exist apart from you.
- My development and wholeness do not matter.
- I don't really exist. I'm not real. I have no right to exist. I don't deserve to live.
- I am incapable and incompetent. I can't do it.
- I can't keep commitments or attain my goals.
- I can't acquit my responsibilities to others.
- I must avoid anything uncomfortable. I avoid conflict and hard work. I am too weak to face confrontation or hold boundaries.

With these beliefs that you developed as a child, you have grown into the Pushover. Your undermining beliefs now show up in your adult behaviours.

Wounded Behaviour of the Pushover Archetype

- I am **not important**. I don't have meaning.
- I feel invisible and treat myself as invisible.
- I don't feel real. I don't feel like I really exist. I am not an adult. I am still a child. I am indistinct, not properly formed.
- I am worthless. "I don't matter". I am not significant. I am different from you. You matter. I am deficient.

> *"A person is in hell who has lost his self-esteem."*
> Robert Schuller

- I have **no power**. I am weak-willed. "**I give up**". I'm knocked back by difficulties. I have no faith in myself. I am not consistent, steady, or determined. I am easily manipulated. I can't stand the pain. I collapse. I become wretched and helpless.
- "I can't get up", "I can't do it". I can't get out of bed. I can't get to work on time. I'm lazy and inactive. I can't work hard.
- I lack energy. I'm so exhausted. I am depleted and defeated.
- I'm just not capable or effective. I can't do my job properly.
- I never have any time for myself. I give away my time to others.
- I'm trapped in awful work that I hate. It's so dull it's killing me. I don't know how to do anything else. I can't change my job.
- I **don't like myself**. I don't think much of myself.
- I am unsure about my self-image. I don't have a stable or clear identity. I try to build my identity around how different I am from everyone else.
- I am living with a fantasy self I have built up. I try on different identities over time. I try identities I think others will like but I am uncertain about who I actually am.
- I am tied up by the conditioning of my childhood and cannot see myself outside of it.
- I nurse and hold onto old wounds and pain from the past. I dwell on my negative feelings towards those who have hurt me.
- My sense of self is so brittle that I'm susceptible to criticism, rejection or slights. I try to puff myself up, but I am afraid you don't respect me or think much of me.

> *"I've got a bad case of the 3:00 am guilts –*
> *you know, when you lie in bed awake*
> *and replay all those things you didn't do right?*
> *Because, nothing solves insomnia like a nice warm glass*
> *of regret, depression and self-loathing."*
>
> D.D. Barant

- I **can't get angry**. I don't need anger. Anger is wrong. It's bad as it leads to violence.
- My hidden anger slips out sideways when I'm passive-aggressive, judgmental and sarcastic. The anger I do have is anger at myself.
- I am moody, take everything personally, self-absorbed and hypersensitive.
- I am flat, emotionless. I don't have any feelings at all. I am emotionally constricted and feel a bit inhuman, and impersonal.
- I am rigid, and I keep my passions, feelings, and impulses in check. I won't follow my instinctive drives. I am controlled and inflexible. I repress myself.
- I can't be childish, and I won't release myself into fun. I am uneasy when others are playful and try to stop them from messing around with puritanical judgments.

> *"To one's enemies:*
> *"I hate myself more than you ever could."*
>
> Alain de Botton

- I lack courage. I cannot hold a boundary. I can't say no and mean it.
- I'm physically abused, bullied, and afraid of punishment. I avoid confrontation. I'm a **victim**. I'm picked on, betrayed, a martyr.
- I don't recognise the enemy. I can't tell when someone is trying to take advantage of me. People walk all over me. It's not fair.
- I am afraid of being harmed. I am so scared you will hurt me. I am worried that you will try and control me, yet I want you to rescue me.
- I am ashamed of myself. To avoid my shame, I try to humiliate or belittle others.
- I am so overwhelmed, so tired and drained.
- If you do try to help me, I will drive you away. I am useless, a hopeless case. I torment myself. I break down. I want to kill myself.
- It's always me that's blamed. It's my fault. I couldn't help it. I can't ever get it right. I always mess it up. It's better that I don't start at all.

"Why are you lying awake, thinking that you're a terrible person?
To keep my mind occupied when I can't sleep.
Some people count sheep. I self-loathe."

Rainbow Rowell

- I **can't love** you. I cannot cope with what it would do to me if you rejected me or used my love against me. You would crush me. I am not strong enough for that.
- I am afraid that you are going to reject me. To protect myself, I abandon you first.
- I withhold and avoid relationships. Relationships involve conflict and difficulties, and I don't want that. I run away from commitment. I am the lone wolf.
- I am worthless. No one would want to be around me. I am not worthy of love.
- I think other men are trying to get something from me or get one over me. Men scare me, so I try not to be around them.
- I can't bear being unsure of myself, so I shut down. Now I can't get so hurt, or at least you won't see when I've been hurt.
- I don't do emotions. I am insensitive and emotionally shallow. Nothing touches me.
- I have loveless sex. I use sex to de-stress.
- The unacknowledged pain of my childhood haunts me. I hide this pain from the world. I am scared of failing, just like my father did before me.

"I guess I felt attached to my weakness.
My pain and suffering too.
If I like these things, why should I apologise?"

Haruki Murakami

- I **refuse to take responsibility**. The world is against me.
- I am full of **self-pity**. It never goes right for me. The world is to blame. I need to take care of myself because life is so hard for me. It's not fair. It's not my fault.
- I am dissatisfied. I am not happy with life. I am not happy with myself.
- I'm attached to disappointment. I don't see the good in my life. I long for what I cannot have. I will never be fulfilled, grateful or satisfied. I cannot allow myself to experience the good in life. If I did, I would lose my identity as a suffering victim. I cling to my old story of myself.
- I give myself to anyone in authority. I have to justify myself to leaders. I let old, learned voices tell me what to do. I don't trust my inner authority.
- I project onto authority figures and put them on a pedestal. I expect them to be great and perfect at all times. If they are not, I moan and criticise them behind their backs. I complain about the company to fellow workers but won't say anything at meetings.

> *"Self-pity in its early stages is as snug as a feather mattress.*
> *Only when it hardens does it become uncomfortable."*
> Maya Angelou

- I am **resentful,** dissatisfied and disappointed. I am not respected, appreciated or recognised.
- I have been wronged. This is unjust. I am oppressed.
- My bitter attitude pushes people away, so I find others who are resentful and congregate with them.
- My negative, constrictive attitude erodes my creative powers and corrodes any richness or fulfilment I might have enjoyed.

> *"Those demons crawled again under my blanket, and they joined me in bed,*
> *They sang me a song of sorrows, wars, and all those flashbacks*
> *that fuck up the peace of my head."*
> Samiha Totanji

- I am **unreliable** and flaky. I can't focus, have poor self-discipline, and don't follow through. I fail to build, won't change what I'm worth, and can't complete.
- I cannot sustain consistent employment and don't honour my financial responsibilities. I never have enough money. I can't fully support myself or those who depend on me.
- I am so impractical and unproductive. I won't be real, get down to work, or produce results. I complain that "I shouldn't have to do this". I was made for better things than this.
- I struggle. I drop balls all the time. I am juggling, and I can't keep it all going. I'm endlessly making mistakes.

> *"You can't give real responsibilities to the shady shoulders.*
> *The weak may learn, but a shady person will always fall flat on their face."*
> Sarvesh Jain

The Pushover Speaks

Each paragraph is the voice of a different man.

"It's not funny, and it's not fair. I'm not important. I don't matter. I am the biggest underachiever on the planet. My shoulder hurts, I am tired, I hate my job. I should get out more. I complain about everything. I'm not fully a man."

"I did not have any training to be a Warrior. I am immature. I still feel like a boy. I don't have discipline, control or focus. If I don't succeed easily, I abandon the project.
I will only work at what I am competent at. I keep my boundaries unclear so I can please and rescue. I make sure we get along by avoiding conflict and confrontation.
I don't upset people because they won't like me. Anger is not allowed, as it might hurt someone. I don't work to my full potential. I don't keep commitments to myself or others."

"I can't find a place to live. I am downsizing. I can't get regular work. I'm burned out.
I can't be consistent. I'm a failure. I am inadequate.
I can't support myself as I want to."

"The goalposts are changing again. I am despondent, deflated, on lockdown.
I want to run away. I'm daunted by what is coming next. I'm feeling less than.
I'm not valued enough. I'm not seen enough. I'm not recognised enough."

"Nothing matters. There's a huge vacuum where I thought I could be.
There's nothing. I draw in a breath, then give up. I can't act. I'm completely paralysed.
I quit everything. I'm inert. I try to move forward, but I'm shackled.
It's safer to do what other people want me to do so I can be what they want me to be."

"I'm not really here. I am an automaton. I just can't get through life. I don't want to be here.
I am afraid of anger. I'm not meant to be angry. What am I here for?
I am not important in life.
I don't like myself."

"I am small, vulnerable, weak. I am inept. I don't want to be seen. I want to hide away.
I am disempowered, lacking, lethargic, lazy. I ignore what needs to be done.
I pity myself."

"Bullies scare me. They want to fuck me up. If I stand up to a bully, he will like it, so I don't stand up. I just walk away.
When I get to the top of the mountain, then there's another, and another, then I die. It's all shit."

"I don't follow through or complete. I'm weak-willed. I duck my financial obligations.
I owe money. I never have enough money."

"It's a battle to engage my will. I give up on myself. I feel defeated. I whinge. I hide away.
I let others do the work for me."

"I'm stuck.
I'm a bit of a ghost.
A bit ephemeral.
I'm insubstantial, weak, nothing."

"I utterly defer to those who are powerful. I do what I am told. I am cowardly, timid.
I am terrified of criticism. I shrink from judgement. I am a coward. I bury myself in the soil and get trampled, trodden on.
Then I feel even more sorry for myself."

"I'm too weak to do it. There's no point. I don't have any authority. I only do something when I'm told to. Even then, I get it wrong. So, I hide, stay quiet, ride it out.
I know there is no point in doing anything.
Anything I do will be criticised, ineffective."

"I want to rest, to rot. I am tired. I want to stay safe. I feel very, very vulnerable. If I try, I will fail. I don't enjoy being here. I am not wanted. I won't step into anything. A little difficulty and I give up. I try to avoid trouble."

"I can't get out of bed. I want to, but I can't. I'm weighed down. My body is really heavy.
I can't focus on work. I know I need to do this, but I can't focus. I'm frustrated. I'm shit."

"I am nice. I don't trust anger. I don't trust power. I live with regret. What other option is there?"

Anger and your Healthy Warrior

*"Anybody can become angry — that is easy,
but to be angry with the right person and to the right degree
and at the right time and for the right purpose, and in the right way
— that is not within everybody's power and is not easy."*
Aristotle

Anger is a powerful emotion and needs to be managed skilfully by your Healthy Warrior. When used with care, it is a vital force that your Warrior can master to move your life forward. Misused, it causes pain, destruction and broken relationships.

As with all emotions, anger cannot be suppressed or ignored for long. If you disregard and try to squash your anger, it will disappear into your shadows so that you no longer have conscious control over it. Just because you are not aware of your anger does not mean that you are not angry. It just means that your anger breaks out in ways you do not intend, such as being passive-aggressive, sarcastic, or suddenly bursting into rage.

Your healthy Warrior can work with your anger in several ways.

Self-definition

*"Transformation is my favourite game, and in my experience,
anger and frustration are the result of you not being authentic
somewhere in your life or with someone in your life.
Being fake about anything creates a block inside of you.
Life can't work for you if you don't show up as you."*
Jason Marx

Your healthy Warrior defines himself by your successful actions. He is responsible for your healthy ego, the platform of yourself that you stand on to engage with the world.

To maintain your healthy ego, your Warrior must assert the boundary of yourself. Your Warrior can clearly define what is you and what is not you.

Your healthy Warrior may face situations where your solid sense of self is questioned or threatened. In these situations, he can use the force of your firm, steady, healthy anger to hold the boundary and demarcation of yourself. Here he uses your anger as a force for honourable self-protection and healthy self-definition.

Establishing and Protecting Clear Boundaries

*"Anger is the deepest form of compassion, for another, for the world, for the self, for a life, for the body, for a family and for all our ideals,
all vulnerable and all, possibly about to be hurt.
Stripped of violent reaction, anger is the purest form of care,
the internal living flame of anger always illuminates what we belong to,
what we wish to protect and what we are willing to hazard ourselves for."*
David Whyte.

Your Healthy Warrior is responsible for protecting your realm. It is his job to establish a clear boundary around your life so that you can identify and defend all who are within your domain.

If your boundary is broken, your Warrior can step up to stop whatever is breaking your border and restore it to full effectiveness. He can use the force of your healthy anger to protect your kingdom and all in it and to restore your disrupted boundary to maximum effectiveness.

If your Warrior is alert, he can take immediate action, with healthy anger, if necessary, to correct and restore. His timely response will mean that he does not need to take more robust measures, such as resorting to violence later.

Protection

*"Love implies anger.
The man who is angered by nothing cares about nothing."*
Edward Abbey.

Your healthy Warrior honourably protects the weak. With healthy, appropriate, balanced, and merciful anger, he steps forward to prevent injustice and stop abuse and cruelty. He does this for himself as well as for others. He tried to stop others from getting hurt. He tries to provide a social environment that is safe and fair.

Anger can show up as defence when we are attacked. With anger, we face the immediate reality of the threat rather than allowing our fear to persuade us to ignore or run away from it. With our courage fuelled by appropriate anger, we confront the situation to stop the damage immediately. We directly address the hurt, so it does not infect us. Our anger equips us to stand up for ourselves and others with robust and peaceful determination so that we cannot be moved or shaken. It does not need to be aggressive. It does not need to threaten. Instead, it can form a rock-solid, implacable force that monitors and maintains firm, clear, reasonable boundaries. It can protect without hurting.

Being True and Speaking The Truth

*"Bitterness is like cancer. It eats upon the host.
But anger is like fire. It burns it all clean."*
Maya Angelou

Your healthy Warrior seeks to speak your truth, no matter how difficult the situation he faces. Each time he speaks his truth, he defines himself further. He can use his anger to support himself to speak out when it would be easier for him to keep quiet. He can strengthen himself when he chooses to go against perceived wisdom and when he needs to stand separate and differentiate himself from others. His anger supports him to be distinct and unique, even if his way is not popular.

Anger as Strength

> *"A man that does not know how to be angry*
> *does not know how to be good."*
> Henry Ward Beecher

Your healthy Warrior knows that your anger has strength and possibility. When your Warrior has easy access to your anger, you know that you can respond without being constrained by fear. Your strength means that the more vulnerable and gentle parts of yourself can relax, knowing they will always be protected. Your Warrior strength gives you the power to be yourself and face and deal with the truth, no matter how difficult.

Your anger has a dial, and you can adjust its volume according to the situation you find yourself in. You can adapt to match the anger that is coming toward you. If your anger is not acknowledged, then you can raise its pitch and its power until it is strong enough to clear up the situation that called it forth.

Dealing with Conflict

> *"There's nothing wrong with anger, provided you use it constructively."*
> Wayne Dyer

Your healthy Warrior uses your intense balancing anger to give you the strength and courage to deal with conflict and difficult conversations. As the Warrior, you step up to remind others, and yourself if necessary, of the agreements they have made and ask them to hold themselves accountable if they break those agreements.

Your anger gives you the strength to sit with conflict and guide yourself and others out of danger. It gives you the power to unearth underground currents and bring deception and abuse to light. It gifts you the strength to stand still and firm in situations of darkness and threat.

Anger is bravery. Channelling anger to deal with conflict requires the courage to stand and face difficulty. To have the power to express anger is empowering. Anger is grounded in inner strength and steadfastness. With appropriate anger, you can bring about change and gain restitution and justice. With access to anger, you can overcome difficulties and survive danger.

Anger as life-force

> *"If you try to get rid of fear and anger without knowing their meaning,*
> *they will grow stronger and return."*
> Deepak Chopra

Anger keeps you moving. It prevents you from freezing with fear. It provides courage and gives extra resources of energy. It moves towards, and it spreads outwards. It helps you get up when you fall. It brings bright focus and directed intent. It helps you repair and heal so that you can step up and take your place again. It fires up your mission and brings dogged strength to your purpose. It has many manifestations, from slow and smoking to clean, bright and fiery.

Anger must be felt

> "Anger is like flowing water;
> there's nothing wrong with it as long as you let it flow.
> Hate is like stagnant water;
> anger that you denied yourself the freedom to feel, the freedom to flow;
> water that you gathered in one place and left to forget.
> Stagnant water becomes dirty, stinky, disease-ridden, poisonous, deadly;
> that is your hate.
> Allow yourself to feel anger; allow your waters to flow.
> Be human."
> C Joybell C

Anger is movement, and when you feel it entirely, you can then move on. There is no need to let it linger if you express it appropriately. Anger only hangs around when you don't express it.

Many men have been wounded by inappropriate anger that hurt them as children. Many have not witnessed the appropriate use of healthy anger. Without a model and example of healthy anger, men are likely to behave in two possible ways:

1). They manifest the dangerous anger they have seen modelled.

2). They decide that anger is wrong and dangerous and that they will never exhibit the anger they saw as a child. They try to eliminate their anger.

Neither of these approaches is healthy. A healthy approach is to practice and become familiar with anger and use it as a powerful tool.

Anger and the Pushover

When a man has Too Little Warrior, he is likely to tell himself that he has no anger. He may believe that anger is harmful, destructive or morally deficient. While he tells himself he has no anger, it shows up as passive aggression and wounding underhand criticism.

Lacking in Anger

With no access to healthy anger, a man is likely to become a victim of others' anger.

Without anger, a man abandons himself because he cannot marshal any strong defence or stop others from walking over his boundaries.

Without anger, a man lacks clear self-definition, which leaves him without a distinct sense of self, making it very hard for him to be sure of himself.

Anger is a powerful energetic force, and without it, a man is in danger of living a passive life that lacks fire and strength. He may then suffer from depression and excess fear. He may tend to weakness and being a victim. He may blame others, be bored and jaded, indifferent to the juice of life. He may become deeply inauthentic, passive and avoidant. He may manifest many of the behaviours of the weak, ineffectual victim so that he accomplishes little and instead languishes in the shadows of his life.

Anger and the Bully

When we are in the part of us that is an overblown Warrior, we are likely to feel way too much anger. We are bubbling over with anger that feels out of control and threatening to the people around us. It often shows up as explosive rage and fury.

The Bully is likely to feel all his emotions as anger. When he feels fear or sadness, these show up as anger.

Too much anger

The Bully exhibits constant anger, fury, and cycles of rage, then guilt, followed by further explosions. He constantly resorts to violence and brutality. He uses his anger to abuse others and to burn himself. He throws his anger all about and gives way to a rampage of rage.

The Bully creates boundaries that are way too harsh and strong, and he polices them over vigorously. At the same time, he thoughtlessly breaks through others' boundaries and then refuses to acknowledge the truth of what he has done.

He seeks to create fear by trying to control the world with his bullying anger.

These are some of the ways the Bully uses anger against others:

- He angrily overrides others when they point out the truth.
- He doesn't listen, jumps to conclusions, and demands immediate action.
- He is impetuous and irritable, reacts irrationally and explodes over small things.
- He takes unacceptable risks and fantasises about violence.
- He has ulcers and skin problems like eczema.
- He cuts and hurts himself.
- He damages his property to vent.
- He is prone to rage and takes his anger out on the innocent.
- His smile is false; he avoids eye contact, withdraws, has headaches, sore muscles and a clenched jaw.

Part 5

The Lover

Introduction

> "A flower cannot blossom without sunshine, and man cannot live without love."
> Max Muller

Oh, the Lover! The beautiful, sensitive, vulnerable, connected, emotional Lover. In many ways, the Lover holds the essence of life. Here, much like the King, it's about being fully in every moment. But here, unlike the King, it is not about holding and stewarding; it's about connecting and relating. The magic of relationship fascinates, captivates and occupies our Lover.

How did it feel to you to read our Lover's opening lines? For me, before I looked at myself, I would never have considered myself beautiful, sensitive, emotional, and, least of all, vulnerable. Sadly, for men, particularly in the past, boys were conditioned and socialised from an early age not to express feelings. In the patriarchal system, boys were taught not to show tender feelings or emotions. They were especially conditioned not to cry.

Men who cannot access their emotions and don't feel much miss out on depth and quality in life. They do not love their partners as deeply or fully as they could. They miss much of the incredible, intimate closeness they could have had with their children.

It's not just men. As Robert Johnston says that "our wounded feeling function, probably the most common and painful wound which occurs in our Western world. It is very dangerous when a wound is so common in a culture that hardly anyone knows that there is a problem".

> "Underneath it all we are tribal individuals.
> We seek connection because we need to know
> we are not alone on this planet."
> Gabrielle Roth.

Human beings are social animals. We evolved this way to survive since the beginning of the human race, and this inner human social system lives inside us still. We are tuned in to the emotions and feelings of the people around us, and we unconsciously respond to the moods of the groups we are involved with. We automatically assess our position in the group and measure our worth from how people treat us. As a result, we behave in ways acceptable to our society and hide and repress our darker primitive desires in our shadow personality.

As social beings, we know that the bonds we develop with others are essential for our survival and happiness. We need social attention to feel alive. Eye contact confirms our existence, and the attention we receive lets us know that we are appreciated and known for who we are. Attention confirms our self-worth, so we are motivated to get attention. We crave validation from others.

> *"A friend is one to whom one may pour out the contents of one's heart,
> chaff and grain together, knowing that gentle hands will take and sift it,
> keep what is worth keeping, and with a breath of kindness,
> blow the rest away."*
> George Eliot

Thinking helps bring us facts and objective data, but it gives little sense of inner worth. Feelings give a sense of worth, meaning and value. It's our feelings that make us truly human. When we give all value to thinking and suppress our feelings, we are in danger of impoverishing our existence. Without relatedness, connection, warmth, generosity, and loving feelings, we lead less of a life, lonely, and lacking in meaning. When feelings are impotent and numb, the natural, instinctual man dies. Idealism and love wither. We become hard. Life loses its flavour even if we are doing well and being successful.

Our Lover holds and expresses the feeling part of ourselves, and because we grew up in a harsh world, most of us were wounded early in this archetype. Maybe our sensitivity was damaged during childhood by an ultra-masculine environment or because we were persecuted for gentleness or sexual orientation. Maybe you were told that your sexuality was sinful and must be suppressed if you are to be connected to Spirit. Whatever happened, we all lost our innocence and left the Garden of Eden.

Our Healthy Lover determines our capacity to relate and love, so attacks on our expressive feeling vitality harden us. We harden by putting up protective defences between ourselves and the world, stopping ourselves from feeling and making ourselves partly numb. Feeling less makes it hard for us to feel alive, relate, have fulfilling relationships, and feel passionate. Many of us men end up subduing our Lover's life force and, in the process, suppressing our capacity and ability to love.

> *"In the sweetness of friendship
> let there be laughter,
> and sharing of pleasures.
> For in the dew of little things
> the Heart Finds Its Morning
> and Is Refreshed."*
> Kahlil Gibran

Being numb makes it hard to make sense of all of this. For me, it was as if I could not read the words and did not have the language. "I'm fine. I've got feelings." I did not know that I was not feeling much.

It is unnatural for human beings not to feel emotions. All humans have feelings, so if we are taught to suppress and not express them, they sit inside us, unexpressed, lodged in our being. Feelings articulate what it is to be alive, to live in a challenging world. What we do not express outwardly runs around under our surface.

Just because I am not able to cry doesn't mean that I am not sad. It just means that my sadness is out of reach. It cannot flow, be felt and move on. It sits in me, an ocean of sadness, and the extent to which I cannot feel represents the distance I am from life. In time it forms an underground life of its own; lost, forgotten, and lonely. The bigger it gets and the longer it lasts, increases its downward pull. I may find myself slowly, reluctantly being dragged down into its heavy, depressed, unexpressed depths without realising what's happening.

> *"It is being with the other that makes the unbearable bearable,*
> *the adverse favourable, the ugly beautiful, the disenchanted enchanted,*
> *the disconnected or fragmented whole.*
> *It is when I am with you that I feel this project of being alive is truly worthwhile and for you I am willing to endure the unendurable,*
> *because in your eyes I see God and my life becomes something worthy,*
> *noble and perhaps even beautiful."*
> Stephen Anthony Farah

In my own personal development, feelings, especially sadness, have been the last area I have slowly, tentatively approached. During the 1960's and 1970's, the society I grew up in discouraged boys from showing their feelings. We were encouraged to be tough. In school, we were repeatedly beaten.

As boys, we policed each other. We expected each other to endure being caned without showing any distress or feeling. The worst possible thing we could do was cry. Once I walked into a class after lunch, still chewing a sandwich. The teacher immediately hauled me to the front and caned me twice, really hard. Because I was not prepared and had not clamped down on my feelings, and because of the shock of how hard he hit me, a tear rolled out of my left eye as I walked through the boys to my desk. That tear marked me as soft, and I was teased about it for weeks.

As an adult, I have found it extremely hard to cry. Before I started attending to my development, the only time I wept openly was when my beautiful dog was run over and killed.

When I cry, I feel extremely uncomfortable. As soon as I start crying, a mechanism inside tries to get me to stop. I seize up. I try to suck all the tears and sorrow back inside so it does not show.

> *"Emotion is the chief source of all becoming conscious.*
> *There can be no transforming of darkness into light*
> *and of apathy into movement without emotion."*
> C G Jung

This inability to cry was a symptom of my broader and deeper numbness. Conditioned not to feel sadness or fear, I clamped down on all my feelings as a child. My childhood was damaged by living in a brutal war, and at the age of fifteen, I lost my country and every friend I had when we left Africa and emigrated to the United Kingdom. Although this move broke my heart and filled me with immense sadness, I hardly felt it at the time. I have lived my life floating over an ocean of frozen inner sorrow. It is only in recent years that I have been able to feel this grief inside and slowly, tentatively, express it, little by little.

My inability to express sadness was the most obvious symptom of my general emotional numbness. In relationship after relationship, I encountered frustration from my partners due to my lack of feelings and expression. I found this very confusing.

I buried myself in work throughout my life, which helped me not feel much. When I work, I am in Warrior, busy doing but feeling little. When something needs to be done, it is easy for me to put my feelings aside. One emotion I can easily express is Warrior anger. Actually, I would convert all emotions to anger. I would show sadness and fear as anger. Instead of feeling sad or afraid, I would explode and lash out. I would punch or break things. I would never do this to people. I know what it is like to be attacked and bullied. I don't want that for anyone else and would try to protect others from abuse. But I could not cry. I learned that to cry is to be weak, and so I would be angry instead. Anger is one emotion that our society generally, within bounds, allows boys and men to express. It was the only emotion I could express easily. I would vent all of my feelings as anger. I overrode my sadness, pain and fear and was endlessly angry.

> "When it's time to suffer, you should suffer;
> when it's time to cry, you should cry.
> Cry completely.
> Cry until there are no more tears
> and then recognize in your exhaustion that you're alive.
> The sun still rises and sets. The seasons come and go.
> Absolutely nothing remains the same and that includes suffering.
> When the suffering ends, wisdom begins to raise the right questions."
> Seido Ray Ronci

Many broken relationships later, my children came along. I have a son and a daughter, and their arrival changed me. The love they showed me warmed a frozen part inside. I absolutely love them and never held back from them in any way. With them, I felt safe to be emotional. I did not want them to have a numb, distant father. I sought to surround them with love and connection. I wanted them to feel free to express their emotions, including fear and sadness, without conditioning them out of these emotions. I wanted them to be healthy emotionally. I could not model this for them when I was numb myself.

Inspired by my children's love, I followed the long, painful journey to feel again. It has taken a long time. I had to re-approach areas of my life where I did not feel, where sadness just got stuck and lodged inside. I have felt into my old pain and expressed it. I have done this gradually and slowly, and I am still here to tell the tale! I haven't fallen apart because I cried. I was afraid that, with so much sadness inside, I might never be able to stop if I expressed it. I haven't been ridiculed or judged for crying. I have been respected and loved even more, and I have been able to feel love more and more as I expressed my feelings. As I have slowly worked my way into my deep emotions, I have come more fully alive. I feel myself! I am alive!

The gift of allowing ourselves to feel is to be fully alive. I can only share myself with others when I am fully alive.

And so, to the Lover.

"E-NOUGH.
Stop shaming feelings of anger, of doubt, of depression and guilt.
Stop it.
It is not 'less than', it is not lower vibration.
It is not.
It is our human experience in full glory.
It is the vastness of our nature.
It just IS.

And the biggest tribute to the soul is to merge with that vastness.
To have the fucking tits or balls to feel what you feel.
Whatever it is.
Whatever.
Move with that energy.
Don't blame others.
Don't blame yourself.
Just feel.

Hear the intelligence of these feelings.
They are guides.
Visiting you in full trust of your essence: infinite love.
Dark guides that are just as sacred as our Light guides.
Let them visit you.
Let their intelligence speak.
Let their loyal visits remind you of how relentlessly they invite you to embrace them.
Even if you don't.

Be radically present with yourself.
Be with the resistance, be with the openness.
Be with the bliss, be with the dirt.
Be.

And fuck anyone that tells you to 'suck it up', 'to change the way you feel in order to heighten your vibration', 'be at peace' when you most certainly feel like fire is blazing out of your belly.
Fuck anyone that tells you how to feel.
I'm am a glorious representation of nature.
I shine, I rain, I thunder, I storm, I am the noise and the silence.

And I will not be anything less to comfort you or your beliefs."

Sharona Lautoe

The Healthy Lover Archetype

*"Don't walk behind me; I may not lead.
Don't walk in front of me; I may not follow.
Just walk beside me and be my friend."*
Albert Camus

Behaviours of the Healthy Lover Archetype

- I live a vibrant, passionate life.
- I am **life force,** descended from the divine into the human, creatively energising and animating. I am libido, not just sexual appetite, but love for life, life instinct itself.
- I am the primal energy of life, of aliveness, passion, and intensity.
- I live in the now, with enthusiasm and happiness, present in the moment.

*"Friendship is an obstetric art; it draws out our richest and deepest resources;
it unfolds the wings of our dreams and hidden indeterminate thoughts;
it serves as a check on our judgements, tries out our new ideas,
keeps up our ardor, and inflames our enthusiasm."*
Antonin Sertillanges

- I **love people, family, friends, sharing,** and being close and entwined in their lives. I love cooking and making a home for us all. I am always willing to get involved and lend a hand.
- I exercise the law of attraction. I attract others to me, to who I am. They are attracted because they know whatever happens will be good for them. People are drawn to me like bees to honey.
- I want love, connection, and belonging. I want to be close to you. I want to be part of the family and the group. I want to share our common interests and
- our favourite activities.
- I am warm hearted, welcoming and friendly. I am relaxed, easy to get on with and enjoyable to be around.
- I am present, open, and have deep love to give. I seek to please people. I also know when to back off, give space, and let go.

*"So I think I'll dance today to music only I can hear.
And daydream about all the magic inside of me coming out to play.
And have deep conversations where I can look into the eyes of someone I love. And as they
tell me their story, I'll find the hidden wonder in all their little details.
And I'll feel so happy to be alive."*
S.C. Lourie

- I am relaxed and **playful** and give the child inside me space to play.

- I have easy access to laughter, song, dance, touch, comfort, and nurturing.
- I am here to feel and have **pleasure**. I bring and receive pleasure. I move towards pleasure, to expand, to tune in, to connect. I relax into pleasure, opening to new ideas and experiences, to my inner and outer world.
- I accept the pleasure of the moment and know it won't last for long.
- I try to separate from, avoid, and move away from all that brings me pain.
- I connect to the sweet natural **rhythm** of life, that same rhythm that flows through you and me.
- I want to yield to this pleasurable **flow**, go with it, channel it, dive beneath it, and be swept along by it.
- I am flexible, **fluid**, flowing, spontaneous, creative and inspired.
- I am open to exploration, novelty, and change, and I am willing to take risks.

"His hands are holding my cheeks, and he pulls back just to look me in the eye
and his chest is heaving and he says,
"I think," he says, "my heart is going to explode,"
and I wish, more than ever,
that I knew how to capture moments like these and revisit them forever.
Because this.   This is everything."

Tahereh Mafi

- I am **romantic** by nature.
- I am fascinated and absorbed by my love relationship. I base my essence in this relationship.
- I fully expect that my partner will be there for me.
- I am open to depending on my partner and being depended on.
- I effectively manage my impulses and feelings in relationship.
- I healthily maintain my autonomy and independence.
- I am resilient when my relationship faces adversity and challenging times.
- I have good relationships with my parents and other authority figures, as does my partner.
- My partner and I show affection and love to trust and be intimate.
- My partner and I have positive belief systems about ourselves, our families and society.
- My partner and I actively promote robust and secure attachment with each other and our children.
- I love **nature** and love to be outside. I connect with plants and animals. I feel at home in the natural world.

- I feel the natural force that runs below the surface of all life, including my own. I seek to unite this life force in me with the life force in other creatures.
- My **sexuality** is a beautiful expression of my Lover.
- I am Eros, the connecting force that attracts, brings together, and unites. I am the attraction of opposites and their union.
- I form vital connections. I banish isolation. I am the binding force that holds the universe together.
- I am alluring, sensual, and comfortable in my sexuality. I am physically aware, alive to the physical world, and in love with the natural world.
- My sexuality is my life force. I desire, and I am desirable. My penis is my sexual emblem, my blood flowing with my spirit and soul.
- I am in love with passion, pleasure, and desire. I am seductive. I create longing. I am the muse.
- I engage in sex to expand my loving heart, to connect and expand my consciousness.

> "There is a language older by far and deeper than words.
> It is the language of bodies, of body on body,
> wind on snow, rain on trees, wave on stone.
> It is the language of dream, gesture, symbol, memory."
> Derrick Jensen

- I live through **sensation**: sight, touch, taste, and sound. I notice, see, and taste. I am sensitive to and deeply in touch with my environment.
- I am deeply sensual, alive to my body and the wider physical world.
- I love how sensations draw me into their world, where I can find unity. I love to be bound to other lives.
- My sensitivity keeps me compassionate and connected with others as I easily unite with them.
- I am willing to be **vulnerable** and accept that I can't be vulnerable on my own. I am eager to turn up and respond. I let you see me.
- I share myself with those who hear me, and those I trust.
- I feel the pain of life. I feel pain in others. I accept that, at times, life is painful, sad, and challenging. Sometimes I go into the night and endure what I find.
- It is frightening to go into darkness, but I know I need to be with all of me to be genuinely alive.
- I try to feel how I armour myself and where I protect myself. I seek to reveal and empathise with the parts of me that need protecting. With my King protecting these parts, I release any armouring layers that separate me from those I love.

> "Vulnerability is the birthplace of love, belonging,
> joy, courage, empathy, and creativity.
> It is the source of hope, empathy, accountability, and authenticity.
> If we want greater clarity in our purpose or deeper
> and more meaningful spiritual lives, vulnerability is the path."
> Brené Brown

- I **surrender.**
- I flow with my nature, biology, instincts, and feelings.
- I dance with ecstatic life force.
- I nurture myself. I attend to my needs and desires. I care for myself.
- I **don't want boundaries** or limitations. I want to feel and experience the whole world, all at once.
- I step over the boundary of the old into the unprotected field of the new leaving all fixed rules and all limits behind, and I find creativity.
- I don't want social forms and customs to limit me. I will not be constrained by the artificial.
- My life is often messy and unconventional. I am the opposite of Warrior, who wants boundaries and order.
- I don't want to be frowned upon by religions, by spiritual disciplines. I am not a trap, a distraction. My longing is life itself. I am energy and inspiration. My desire passionately pulls me forward.
- I hold the virtue of **temperance**. I balance my desires and my needs and keep them healthy and appropriate.
- I balance my Lover's desires with my Warrior's need for boundaries and order.
- I recognise that some religions see me as distracting or even evil and seek to contain and control me by equating my love of sensual pleasure with Satan. For me, nature and my body are not sinful, just natural.
- Some religions, such as Hinduism, hold and celebrate my erotic qualities, allowing me to sensuously embody all forms of the One who lives within.

> "The human body is the best picture of the human soul."
> Ludwig Wittgenstein

Skills

- I foster, develop, and maintain strong, loving, mature **relationships**. My world is the interpersonal world.
- I take delight in relationships. You are so delightful. I want to be in relationship with you. I appreciate you. I am inspired, touched, moved, excited and ignited by you.
- I am here for relationship. I rejoice in the love and connection we create together. I love that in our relationship, each is free to be themselves.

- I love to be loved, needed, wanted and appreciated. I create life as vibrant and deliciously human.
- I am **socially skilled.**
- I love to be around people. I love to socialise, be helpful, and let others know they are loved and appreciated.
- I am diplomatic and charming. I act well when I need to.
- I am sociable. I live through relationships. Spending time with others fills me with energy.
- I am comfortable in my skin. I express grace in my movements and my body.

> "If I had a flower for every time I thought of you,
> I could walk in my garden forever."
> Alfred Lord Tennyson

- I have a **wide emotional range** and easy access to empathy and sympathy. I naturally pick up others' emotions and feel their effect on me. I am emotionally fluent.
- I am comfortable with deep emotion. I feel my sadness, my grief, my loss. I experience the joy of life and all the pain of life as well. I feel this in you as well as in myself.
- I know and feel my emotions, all of them. I am honest with my feelings. I am **sad** at times. I feel my sadness. I don't run away from it. I don't try to understand it. I just feel it. I am a man of sorrow. I know grief.
- I am expressive, dramatic, sensitive and temperamental. I express my emotions and feelings. I flow with strong emotions.
- I want you to respond to my expression.

> "So she thoroughly taught him that one cannot take pleasure without giving pleasure, and that every gesture, every caress, every touch, every glance, every last bit of the body has its secret, which brings happiness to the person who knows how to wake it. She taught him that after a celebration of love the lovers should not part without admiring each other, without being conquered or having conquered, so that neither is bleak or glutted or has the bad feeling of being used or misused."
> Hermann Hesse

- I am fully in touch with my **body** and love to display it. I am beautiful.
- I am profoundly sensual, and I love the pleasure my body brings me and others. I love my body without shame, and I inhabit it to connect with other bodies.
- I want to **touch** and be touched. I want to bind into another. To be physically close feels right.
- I want to touch everything, emotionally and physically. Touching connects me from the inside.
- When I am fully in my body, my restless mind settles. I am in the moment.

- I love to move, to be alive in pleasure, sensation, touch, and movement.

> *"Forget not that the earth delights to feel your bare feet
> and the winds long to play with your hair."*
> Khalil Gibran

- I love to **help and serve others**. Often my work revolves around helping people. I help them to be happier.
- I am a good parent and care lovingly for the welfare of my family.

Gifts

- I am **love**. My love is hot. It is the source of my mysticism; it brings me into oneness with all, both the light and the dark.
- I am Amor: profound loving union with body, spirit, and soul.
- I am Eros: sexual love, the primal desire to bond and unite with all that is life.
- I am non-erotic brotherly and sisterly love.
- I express my love by helping and caring for you. My love for you warms and heals you. I give love freely and easily.
- I give unselfish unconditional love to you. I go out of my way to help you. I see myself as helpful and concerned for others, and this makes my life meaningful. I love to do good which makes me feel valuable and worthwhile. It is a privilege to be in your life.
- My love flows through the veins of my family.

> *"The song of mystical love embraces all of creation
> as it rings from the human heart and from the heart of the world.
> It is one of the great secrets of humanity, waiting to be lived."*
> Llewellyn Vaughan-Lee

- My **feelings** are my deep knowing. They are my fire for life and keep me connected to the fire of life.
- I am compassionate and empathically connected with all that lives around me. I connect to the world with my feelings rather than with my mind.
- My desire is powerful. My **desire** inspires change towards the new, staying open, staying fully alive, and following my soul's urge to move forward.
- I desire to have fun, give and receive pleasure, and create a magical connection with others.
- I desire new experiences, meeting new people, and making new connections. I am alive in all new beginnings, all new opportunities and possibilities.
- I seek the novel, the unexplored and unexpected.

- I hold all the great hunger in the Kingdom for food, sex, reproduction, relationship, family, and connection.
- My longing is to satisfy this hunger. Fulfilling it brings me happiness.

> "Admit something: Everyone you see, you say to them, "Love me."
> Of course you do not do this out loud,
> otherwise someone would call the cops.
> Still though, think about this, this great pull in us to connect.
> Why not become the one who lives with a full moon in each eye
> that is always saying, with that sweet moon language,
> What every other eye in this world is dying to hear?"
> Hafiz

- I have **energy**.
- I am spontaneous, energetic, restless, impulsive, cheerful, curious and independent.
- I create **connection**, to myself, to you, to the world. Being connected gives my life a sense of meaning.
- I encourage deep relatedness that fulfils our deep desire for love, intimacy, and sacred union.
- I concentrate on the personal. When I am with you, I shine, and I am charming.
- I create unity with you. I love to be fluidly interconnected and interdependent with you so we can both appreciate our essential uniqueness.
- I concentrate on the space between us and seek to encourage the love, connection, and unity that lives there.
- I trust in closeness. I love intimacy. I respond to divine longing and surrender to its irresistible pull. I commit to fulfilling this holy longing.

> "Probably the greatest human skill you can have
> is the ability to take love in and metabolise it.
> That's how you grow".
> George Vaillant

- I am **beauty**, raw, innate beauty. I am the beauty of nature, our heavenly natural world, this Eden within which I am alive. Being beautiful is my highest nature. I demonstrate and exhibit my beauty. I don't hide or subdue it. My beauty is here to be seen.
- I appreciate beauty. I see the beauty in everything. My love is my sensual art.
- I am the source of **creativity** in the Kingdom. For me, creativity is not about doing; it's about being. I don't have to perform or achieve. I flow with the breeze of life.
- I love art, music, and all forms of creativity. Art is the playground of my sensuality. I am the sculptor, the writer, the poet, and the painter.
- I am an **artist**. My art expresses the aliveness I feel. I communicate myself as the source of beauty I am.

- I am a craftsman. I am an artisan. I work with my hands. My beautiful work is my art, my loving, exquisite contribution to the world.

> *"Art is the basic instinct of our soul."*
> Streichman

The Lover Speaks

Each paragraph is the voice of a different man.

"I'm creative, joyous, loving, spontaneous, being myself, expressive, have no boundaries, make everyone light up. I'm alive, liberated, mischievous."

"I am connected to complete, unconditional love and acceptance. Where love is I am. I fall into the arms of love. I trust it. I feel it. It is intuitive, from my heart. Nothing is needed from me other than my vulnerability. I have searched for this and found it."

"I am very, very powerful. I am the driving force taking us through life. I am the one who makes the connections. I am charming. I am available. I make good things happen. I befriend, so I am liked. I create belonging so I can be loved. I am kind. I am loving and I am loved. I carry my playful, loving boy. I carry the grief of my lover. I dance. I sing. I play with children. I feel. I am creative. I am never afraid to create space so that my life can flow. I am connected to all of life. I love so much that at times it hurts.
I hold my grief which can't be healed."

"I love words. I love my children's words. I love how my words affect emotion. I am a beautiful poet."

"I never wash away my tears. I enjoy getting sad. I am deeply moved by my beautiful sorrow."

"I am always present in the connection with others. I am the connection, the drive and desire to be with others. I am the heart in the community, the bond of the family and the embrace of relationship."

"I am open to the energy of the universe, the play between atoms and molecules, the force that brings it all together in this beautiful dance of life."

"I seek out pleasure. I love games, playfulness, interrelatedness, intimacy and sex. I want to be always in the flow, sharing my experience as deeply as possible. I want love and connection, to be in groups or a partnership that is unboundaried. I want union."

"I love rhythm, drumming, music, dance. I express myself through movement and touch, I am sensual and sexual, desirable and desired. I am beautiful and exotic, without shame."

"I connect in so many different ways, but my greatest joy comes from nature and being in natural environments. I love the power of waterfalls, the warmth of the sun, the refreshing rain, feeling the wind on my skin, mountains, seas, trees, insects, animals and birds. I feel blessed and content when in natures presence."

"I want to be seen, wholly and completely. I am vulnerable and able to share my pains as well as my joy, it does not frighten me, nor does it shame me. I am perfect as I am and share myself with passion and joy. To be in this place of sharing is pure bliss."

"I hold the power of balance, feeling deeply into what is appropriate in any given time. I can be totally open and unguarded when it is safe, I can also be suitably demure and coy when it is not appropriate to overshare. This is a gift I bring in being able to sense into the moment, determine what is right for me and those I am in contact with. I hold this skill with ease and without overthinking. I am in tune."

"I am a whale that can dive deeply into the emotional seas, always coming up for air when needed. I am as one with all emotions, none of them are beyond my powers. I can be love, I can be anger, I can be fear and I can be joy. Everything I love I can grieve when it is gone."

Wild Lover Archetype
Too Much Lover

"Sensuality may turn into a feverish hunt for rebirth...
The sexual partner turns into a stand-in for various
dream figures, phantasms in a stage-managed resurrection.
These figures are all agents of immortality
to be conquered or succumbed to many times over."
Alan Harrington

Once again we descend into the underworld so that your Heart King can get to know your wounded Lovers, your Wild Lover who lives in excess Lover, and your Lonely Lover who shies away from all Lover behaviours and feelings.

Now that you have spent time with your Healthy Lover, you can feel how your natural Lover lives in you. Sadly, I have noticed that few men reach adulthood with their Healthy Lover intact. This part of us is acutely affected by a harsh environment, and in the face of criticism, abuse, or violence, quickly becomes wounded, armoured, numb and suppressed.

How a Loving Boy is Wounded

Our sensitive Lover Boy had particular core needs that needed to be honoured to create an environment where he could be fully himself.

These included a need for:

- Authentic and consistent connection.
- Long-term loving, stable, and devoted relationships.
- Opportunities to freely express and be himself.
- Opportunities and encouragement to form safe and secure bonds.
- An honoured and accepted place in his family.
- Freedom to play and enjoy pleasure.

If these core needs were not met, then our Lover Boy would have been wounded. Listed below are some behaviours and experiences that may have harmed him.

Wounding family actions and events

- Neglecting him, refusing hugs and loving closeness, denying affection.
- Isolating him and leaving him alone for long periods.
- Excluding him from family activities, secluding him socially, and restricting access to close family members.
- Ignoring him, not recognising his presence, not noticing his social interactions.
- Punishing or teasing him for engaging socially.
- Preventing him from forming friendships or mixing with peers, forcing him to stay at home or in his room. Banning extracurricular activities.
- Breaking his relationships. Expelling or threatening to force him out of his family.
- Punishing his normal emotions and vulnerability. Expecting him not to cry.
- Modelling inconsistent and conflicting emotions and belittling his needs.
- Teasing and shaming him about his body, telling him he is ugly, criticising his body type or weight, restricting his food or preventing him from eating.
- Denying him health care, dentistry, or socially acceptable clothing. Making him dress and act differently from his peers.
- Sexually abusing him. Encouraging inappropriate sexual behaviour. Exposing him to or encouraging him to participate in pornography.
- Approving substance abuse and supplying him with drugs and alcohol.

Situations like these wound your Lover Boy in his healthy essence. If your Boy fights against these beliefs, he comes to believe the following about himself.

Fighting Against his Beliefs

- There is something wrong with the way I love. I don't love right.
- No one will love me. I am not worth loving. I am not lovable, so I have to love incredibly hard to be loved back.
- Love is not safe. When I love, I will be hurt. Loving will be painful.
- I have to be over focused on my desires. No one else cares about what I need, so I must take care of myself.
- I lack self-control. I must continually follow my impulses.
- I must show an excessive expression of my emotions to demonstrate that I do feel.
- I am acutely oversensitive to my own and others' pain and distress.

In response to these wounded beliefs about himself, our Too Much Lover tries way too hard to prove to the world that he is loving and that he is lovable. This effort shows up in the behaviours listed below.

Wounded Behaviour.

- I feel most alive when I am **intensely emotional**, and I need to be highly emotional all the time. I feel deeply emotional right now.
- My emotions are powerful and dramatic. I spray them all around me. I break open.
- My strong feelings last for hours, or sometimes days and fluctuate wildly. This morning, I am happy and deeply loving, but this evening, I am sad, lonely, and empty.
- I express a lot but nothing shifts or changes, and I stay stuck. I don't heal or evolve.
- I am absorbed in my feelings. I have no detachment, so I can't stand back from any of them. They control me. My emotions rule me. They take centre stage in my life.
- I forget the emotion is passing through me, and I feel like I am the emotion.
- I struggle to achieve intimacy. I act out as the victim or the prince. I manoeuvre my partner with emotional manipulation or seductiveness to get my needs met.

> "She drank my burning kisses up.
> With ravenous thirst and greed.
> She drank the breath from out my breast.
> She fed lust without pause;
> She pressed me tight, and tore and rent
> my body with her claws."
> Heinrich Heine

- I am an **addict**. I act on my impulses and follow my desires.
- I binge. I lead myself and you towards addiction.
- I stuff my feelings with food, drugs, drink, medication, anything not to feel.
- I suffer from compulsions and addictions. I become possessed by the things I love.
- I want the excitement of the perfect high, the ultimate union. There are no boundaries to my search and my efforts to maintain this high.
- I **seek a traumatic connection** with a substance or a person. I am a crisis junkie.
- I emote strongly to prove I can feel, to show I can love. I have big scenes, and hysterical bust-ups.
- I hook into others and have unstable and intense relationships that swing between extremes of idealisation and devaluation.
- I smother my partner as I intensely impose my painful definition of love on our relationship.

> "When we're incomplete, we're always searching for somebody to complete us.
> When, after a few years or a few months of a relationship,
> we find that we're still unfulfilled, we blame our partners
> and take up with somebody more promising.
> This can go on and on--series polygamy—
> until we admit that while a partner can add sweet dimensions to our lives,
> we, each of us, are responsible for our own fulfilment.
> Nobody else can provide it for us, and to believe otherwise
> is to delude ourselves dangerously and to
> program for eventual failure every relationship we enter."
> Tom Robbins

- I **act out sexually**, am sexually seductive and provocative and struggle with sexual addiction. I am promiscuous, "so much sex, so little time". I exploit relationships to gratify my needs. I get bored quickly. I want manic disorientating love.
- I am charged with sexual energy. I blur boundaries. I see every relationship as sexual. I get validation from sexual encounters.
- I am the ultimate Lover. I am searching for the most incredible orgasm, the biggest high. I am not interested in the mundane, and once I see the other as ordinary, I fall out of love and move on. I only want the light side. I am not interested in your hurt or how you struggle. Don't be down when I'm around.
- I have affairs. My relationships are wounding and damaging. I can't say no to sexual opportunities.
- I use my physical appearance to draw attention to myself. I am theatrical and provocative. I am seductive. I promise fantasy sexual fulfilment. I enchant you with my beauty, my sensuality, with the promise of me.
- I have poor relationships with same-sex friends because my sexually provocative style threatens their relationships.
- I am sleazy. I flirt endlessly. No one can resist me. I will have sex with you, and nothing will stop me. I am sexually manipulative and abusive.

> "And so he found himself always in search of the perfect love,
> always unable to find it or sustain it,
> and predisposed to re-enact his mother's bewildering abandonment of him."
> Laurence Bergreen

- I am **attention-seeking**. I'm lively, exciting and dramatic, so everyone focuses on me. I perform and entertain people. I am the life and soul of the party. I have unusual stories to tell. I am great fun until the enmeshed dramas I have pulled you into turn ugly.
- I alienate my friends with my constant demands for their attention. I become upset when I am not the centre of attention.
- I "people please" to get closer to people. I am overly friendly, full of emotion, and overflowing with good intentions.
- I am seductive. I flatter and stroke you. I entice you with my love.

- I become intimate very quickly. Soon I will be meddling in your life and making deep demands on you, all in the name of love. I wear myself out for you, then let you know that you are messing up my life.

> "Ordinary life does not interest me.
> I seek only the high moments."
> Anaïs Nin

- I'm desperate for **constant stimulation**, change, novelty, and excitement. Routine bores me. I initiate projects with great enthusiasm and excitement but become quickly distracted and lose interest.
- I am so restless. I am looking for something, but I don't know what it is. I cannot settle down. I am easily bored.
- I focus wholly on pleasure. I have little impulse control, and I follow my desires without restraint. I don't accomplish anything concrete. I want immediate satisfaction. I can't delay gratification.
- I am a hungry ghost with a huge belly that will never be filled. I fixate on oral activities; eating, drinking, smoking, and talking.
- I am full of fantasy. I am deep within Maya. I dance the dance of pleasurable illusion and cannot escape. I am enthralled with the cycle of pleasure and pain. I roast in the agony and ecstasy of my longings.
- Monogamy bores me. Because I am not centred, rooted or boundaried, I have no calm, masculine centre, no self-created inner joy. For me, wholeness is out there, and I constantly search for it in someone or something else.

> "I made her my everything.
> I didn't realise then that when you make someone your everything,
> when they are gone, you have nothing left."
> K McGahan

- I am searching to **find completion through others**, so I always need to be around people. I hunt for someone special to make me whole. If I can't find completion through another, I feel horribly empty. I will do anything to keep you with me.
- Despite all my efforts, I find it very hard to make and keep a stable **relationship** or friendship.
- My "story" is fragmented. I have very few memories of my parents from when I was young. I say my childhood was loving and positive, but I can't remember specific examples.
- I fear separation and make frantic efforts to avoid real or imagined abandonment. I panic when someone is late. I just can't be alone and need other people to be with me all the time.
- My excessive dependency and possessiveness backfire, resulting in the abandonment that I most fear.
- I continuously demand reassurance and attention from my partners, and I am resentful and angry when I don't get it.

- I swing between dramatic outbursts and pleas for support and forgiveness.
- I struggle with my critical inner voices that relentlessly warn me that I am unlovable and about to lose my partner's love.
- I can't leave situations or relationships that are destructive, abusive, and dangerous. I can't get any distance, perspective or detachment.
- Again and again, I rush headlong into new relationships. I try to get very close, very quickly. I want too much from our relationship. I take from you, not checking that you want to give. I give myself away. I am in too deep, too fast.

> "When you have a persistent sense of heartbreak and gut-wrench,
> the physical sensations become intolerable
> and we will do anything to make those feelings disappear.
> People take drugs to make it disappear,
> and they cut themselves to make it disappear,
> and they starve themselves to make it disappear,
> and they have sex with anyone who comes along to make it disappear
> and once you have these horrible sensations in your body,
> you'll do anything to make it go away."
> Bessel A. van der Kolk

- I am very focused on my own needs and comforts, but I disregard the same for you.
- I cultivate a highly positive view of myself to protect my fragile self, which is vulnerable to slights and rejections.
- I often can't make sense of my relationships. I don't understand why the same things happen again and again.
- I don't have healthy ways to self-regulate, so I use others to regulate my emotions.
- I pretend to be open and transparent but actually struggle to open up to others, trust, or get help. I find it difficult to express myself clearly.
- I am co-dependent. I fixate on you and then become exhausted because I give so much to you. I follow a painful cycle of fixation – > dependency –> suffering rejection –> becoming deeply insecure –> clinging desperately to you –> you further reject me.
- I love to be attached to you. I cling, desperate and needy. I have great expectations of what I will get from you. I sacrifice myself to you. I always put you first, wanting to be loving and unselfish, but I end up resentful because I put you first and now rely on you.
- I am so enmeshed with you that I don't know which are my feelings and which are yours. I take on your emotions and feel that they are my own. I am over involved in you and your life.
- I need you to need me. I flatter you, help you, so you want me around. I try to become indispensable to you, so you rely on me, so you would never consider replacing me. I pretend I am generous and don't need anything from you, but I have huge expectations and want you to satisfy my enormous unacknowledged emotional needs.

> *"Being heartbroken doesn't mean you stop feeling. Just the opposite*
> *— it means you feel it all more.*
> *With your heart in fragments, every sensation is sharper,*
> *every emotion more acute.*
> *Your feelings are enhanced,*
> *like a blind man with an impeccable sense of smell,*
> *or a deaf woman whose eyes can perceive things a normal person would never recognise.*
> *The broken-hearted are the best empaths of all."*
> Julie Johnson

- My **"love" makes you feel "crazy"**. I love to get you flustered and acting crazy when you don't get what you want from me so that you do things you later hate yourself for, which I use against you.
- I take advantage of your love and kindness, see it as weak and vulnerable, and abuse your innocence.
- I need you to concentrate on alleviating my pain. Yet, it will never be enough to make me feel good enough or loved enough no matter what you do. I will always criticise your efforts, so you try to give me more. I want you to work hard to prove your loyalty and affection.
- I love how you feel insecure when I give the attention, I should give to you to others. I enjoy throwing you a few crumbs, so you come back to me, hoping that this time I will change.
- I am a martyr for you. I create needs in you that I must fulfil. I try to surround you, envelope and possess you. I am indispensable to you. Be there for me, or I will become sick, break down, and do something dangerous and crazy.
- I try to fill you with guilt and shame because you made me suffer. You owe me. I will make you hurt because you are so selfish. I undermine and criticise you.

> *"Mania is a wild roller coaster run off its tracks,*
> *an eight ball of coke cut with speed.*
> *It's fun, and it's frightening as hell."*
> David Lovelace

- I am endlessly sick and **continually breaking down**. I am a hypochondriac.
- I am manic, unpredictable, and reckless. I am chaos. Chaos is breathing down my neck.
- My process is so huge it leaves no space. Everyone else has to put their process aside to hold mine.
- I have no masculine ego structures to keep me balanced. I have not differentiated from the tumultuous feminine. I have not resolved my mother issues. I am absorbed in the messy, alluring and enchanting feminine.

> "Compared to bipolar's magic, reality seems a raw deal.
> It's not just the boredom that makes recovery so difficult,
> it's the slow dawning pain that comes with sanity - the realisation of illness,
> the humiliating scenes, the blown money and friendships and confidence.
> Depression seems almost inevitable.
> The pendulum swings back from transcendence in shards,
> a bloody, dangerous mess.
> Crazy high is better than crazy low.
> So we gamble, dump the pills, and stick it to the control freaks and doctors."
> David Lovelace

- I am **floundering** in the wild ocean of my senses and feelings. I am awash, pulled one way, then another. I am so sensitive that I am thrown off balance by the intense sensations of the world.
- I am impulsive, and many of the things I do damage and hurt me and others. I engage in risky sexual behaviours, cut myself, and threaten or attempt suicide. I overspend, abuse substances, drive recklessly, and binge eat.
- I don't try to understand myself or find out why I struggle the way I do. I couldn't bear to find out that I am not lovable. I am afraid I can't love properly. I try so hard to be amazing to prove this is not true. I convince myself that the way I behave is normal. At least I'm alive, really alive!
- There is nothing wrong with me; it's not my fault. I have been abused. I am in bits because of what others have done to me. It's your fault I am so angry and bitter. I did nothing wrong.
- I **don't want limits**. Why would I put limits on my pleasure?

> "I have absolutely no pleasure in the stimulants
> in which I sometimes so madly indulge.
> It has not been in the pursuit of pleasure
> that I have periled life and reputation and reason.
> It has been the desperate attempt to escape from torturing memories,
> from a sense of insupportable loneliness
> and a dread of some strange impending doom."
> Edgar Allan Poe

The Wild Lover Speaks

Each paragraph is the voice of a different man.

"She's single. She's got no boundaries. I really fall for her, such a deep affliction. I revere her, oh how I desire her. I'm in awe of her. I want her attention. I want her around. I place divinity on her."

"She's wise and loving. She tells me she loves me. I fall right in. I become massively possessive. I lock the princess in the tower. I imprison her. I show her how powerful I am."

"If she, latched on to another man who, replaced me. Oh! Intolerable! The horror of it. It's too much. And yet, I did it to her."

"I'm manic. I need to chat about all of it. Endlessly. I need you. I fucking need you so much. I need your validation. I need your attention. When I get your attention, it's delicious, for a while. Then I need more, and more. I need your attention all the time. It's so painful when I'm not getting it. I don't know who I am when I'm not getting it. If you can't see me, I am nothing."

"I'm needy. I need your love. I need to find it. I need you to give it to me."

"I'm a manic weirdo. You are so delicious. I love you. I need to love you all over. And if not you, Another woman, and another. I can't stop. I am never satisfied. I want more, and more. I am so empty. I need you to fill me up."

"Dad has gone. I'm now the man of the house. I defend her. We merge. There are no boundaries. We are constantly merged, and I am responsible for her. I don't know where I begin, and she ends. I don't know how to affirm myself. I don't know where I begin, and I end."

"I have an addictive personality, I always need something to fill the void or numb the emotions. Sometimes nicotine is enough, sometimes food. Other times I need something stronger, drink, drugs, sex, attention, drama. Oh it's so painful all the time, let me do something to help me through it. I'm craving something to help, please!"

"Look at me, I'm amazing, always the biggest personality around, with the wildest stories and most expansive gestures. Look at me! Look at me more! Pay me the attention! Tell me how amazing I am and how much you want to be with me. Tell me again."

"We will find the right partner, the perfect match. We just need to keep looking. So far they've all seemed so good at first but then shown their inevitable flaws. I need someone that can really see me and give me all their attention, I don't want them to be needy, that really turns me off. My love is way too intense for most, I need someone that can handle that."

"I have so much energy flowing through me that I can't maintain any balance. It's immense, such a force, so powerful. I end up burning out, I'm driven by this energy and need to be doing something new and exciting all the time that I can't relax. I break down and collapse, it's the only way I can stop. I end up obsessed with my health, always looking for the next fad that will let me maintain my high intensity. Either that or I focus on all my health problems and make them into big dramatic events."

"It doesn't matter how much I love you, how big my gestures of love are or how much I spend on you, you always end up leaving me. I feel unlovable, like there is something wrong with the way I love."

Lonely Lover Archetype
Too Little Lover

*"The deepest need of man is the need to overcome his separateness,
to leave the prison of his aloneness."*

Erich Fromm

While your Tumultuous Lover emotes to try and prove he is lovable and that he can love, your Too Little Lover accepts and believes that he is not lovable and can't love properly.

As a child, he had the same needs as your Too Much Lover and was wounded by the same family dynamics and events.

Instead of fighting these beliefs, he gives in to them and accepts them as true. Because of this, he comes to believe the following about himself.

Giving in to the Belief

- No one wants to be around me. No one cares about me. I have no friends. I am alone. No one wants to give me attention, affection, or friendship.
- No one loves me or has any feelings for me. I am not lovable. No one could ever love me.
- I am ashamed of how I look. I am ugly. I am different from everyone else.
- I am no good around people. I am awkward socially.
- I am isolated from the world. I am alone. I am not part of any group or community.
- I must fuse with you to be happy. You complete me.
- I am empty and floundering.
- I must put my own needs aside for others. My needs do not matter.
- I must not be vulnerable or show my feelings. If I have feelings, I will get hurt.

Your Too Little Lover believed this as a child, and giving in to these messages, he grows into your Lonely Lover as an adult who exhibits the behaviours listed below.

Wounded Behaviour of the Too Little Lover Archetype

- I am **alone.** I am cut off from myself and others. I am uptight and disconnected.
- I felt abandoned as a child, and I suffer from abandonment now, so I feel cold, alone, and desperate. Although this is my most fundamental pain, I also frequently abandon others.
- I am lonely, shy, timid, isolated and introverted. I try to steer clear of closeness and intimacy and maintain a "safe" distance.
- I am fearful and tense that others may ridicule me. I prefer to spend time with myself.
- I have few friendships, date infrequently, and may not want to marry. I prefer to work alone. I avoid opportunities to be part of my family.
- I won't get involved with someone else unless I am sure they like me.

> "The worst loneliness is not to be comfortable with yourself."
> Mark Twain

- I do not feel loved. No one can love me. I cannot love properly.
- I live in a gloomy world. I live a life of loss, sadness, and abandonment. My world is dreary.
- I confirm my experience by secretly wounding others. I betray and abandon, so they withdraw from me.

> "When loneliness is a constant state of being,
> it harkens back to a childhood
> wherein neglect and abandonment were the landscape of life."
> Alexandra Katehakis

- If I get into **a relationship,** I have a hidden agenda of expecting the same love I give to be returned to me. I give way too much, exhausting myself and leaving myself empty. When I don't get back what I expect, I am devastated and shattered.
- In relationships, I blame the other because I'm constantly reacting out of old wounds. I pour out all my repressed relationship pain and grievances. I blame others for not treating me right. I see you as the one causing me pain. You are the problem.
- I struggle with a deep-seated fear that I will be rejected, so I constantly worry and struggle to trust.
- I have an endless need for approval and reassurance, but it never relieves my doubt, no matter how much I get.
- I cling to my partner and become over-dependent on them.
- I turn my self-doubt, self-criticism and insecurity against myself, which leaves me emotionally desperate.
- I tend to be the pursuer in the relationship.

- I have overly positive projections of my partner and strongly negative views of myself.
- I look down on passion, romantic love, and commitment.
- I prefer isolation and may focus extensively on practical issues.
- If I fear my partner wants to leave me, I divert my attention to other goals and possibilities.
- I tend to withdraw and try to cope on my own.
- I don't seek direct support from my partner but try to gain indirect support by complaining or sulking.
- I hide my vulnerability and try to hide my emotions.
- I ensure I don't attach to someone by choosing an unavailable lover or not fully engaging in the relationship. I often tune out and am seldom fully present.
- In a conflict or argument, I withdraw and avoid any action that will bring a connection.
- I have a cynical, negative view of others that I indulge in to compensate for my self-hatred and low self-esteem.
- I get into a relationship where I can play at being small by being emotionally dependent on my partner. I rely on them, and when they let me down, I crash.

> *"There was no other way to say it.*
> *After being heartbroken for so long, I had made myself completely numb inside. Maybe not from physical pain, but anything emotional, yes."*
> J Salaiz

- I have little Lover energy, so I lack **eros**, and my desire is depleted. I am an impotent lover.
- I am frigid and afraid of sex. I deny myself sexual pleasure and feel guilty about sexuality. I have little interest in sexual experiences and limit sexual connections. I am sexually stale.
- I feel uncomfortable with physical contact and try to limit affectionate exchanges.
- I see sex as a block to my spirituality, so I renounce it and try to rise above it.
- I seldom feel pleasure. I have **put pleasure aside**. It feels tainted, so I regulate it with guilt. I defend myself against pleasure.
- I am a puritan and feel guilt and **shame about pleasure**, so I deny enjoyment to myself and shame and punish others. I predate on myself for wanting it.
- Denying myself pleasure, I set up a terrible hungry craving for it, leading me to addiction. I sneakily engage with pleasure in the shadows, often at the expense of others or myself. Afterwards, I hate myself with guilt and self-cursing shame.
- I can't stop. I want pleasure, and I believe it's bad. I suffer from this split in myself.
- I try to suppress all passion and excitement as childish. I control it with my will. I won't desire. I tell myself pleasure is not important.
- I won't admit it to myself, but I long to be loved and touched. Without this, I turn to oral activities for comfort.

> "And though the coldness I have always felt leaves me,
> the numbness doesn't and probably never will.
> This relationship will probably lead to nothing... this didn't change anything."
> Bret Easton Ellis

- I am **socially uncomfortable** and ill at ease in company. I avoid socialising or interacting with others if I can. I believe people don't want to be around me. My belief confirms that I am not worthy of love and friendship.
- I find social occasions hard work and tiring. I am self-conscious. I try to watch and plan everything I say and do. I want to say the right thing, but I am not sure what that is.
- I am socially inhibited, socially inept, unappealing, and inferior. Because of this, I am very sensitive to what you think about me. I fear disapproval, criticism, and rejection. I am always wondering if you can see how awkward and uncomfortable I am. I ask myself if you are judging me like I am judging myself?
- I am so self-conscious. I know my social anxiety is irrational, but I can't stop it. I avoid looking into others' eyes, speaking in public, meeting new people, or being the centre of attention. I use drugs and alcohol to feel confident in social situations.
- I don't want to rock the boat. I cannot handle discord, disagreements, and arguments.
- I express myself in ways others find 'odd' and strange. People see me as eccentric.

> "And what if---what are you if the people who are supposed to love you
> can leave you like you're nothing?"
> E Scott

- I **don't want intimacy**, so I avoid close relationships with others, including my family. I am afraid no one will want me because I am not worth being loved, so I avoid the possibility.
- I am emotionally cold towards others.
- I am irritable and touchy and take everything personally. People step away from me, which makes me even more sensitive, so I am constantly disappointed.
- I fall out with others, but I am always the wronged party.
- I prefer to be alone. I choose to live without interference from others.
- I believe relationships will be complicated and painful and that they will limit my freedom.

> *"Why do people have to be this lonely? What's the point of it all?*
> *Millions of people in this world, all of them yearning,*
> *looking to others to satisfy them, yet isolating themselves.*
> *Why? Was the earth put here just to nourish human loneliness?"*
> Haruki Murakami

- I **dream of love** instead of experiencing it. I fantasise about love while I am cut off from loving relationships and intimacy.
- My sexual life is not real. I watch porn and masturbate rather than have sex.
- I learned to dream like this when I was a child and could not connect with my mother or get the love I wanted from her.
- I am **dry** and stoical. I am wooden, dull, and depressed. I am flat.
- I am undercharged, not truly alive. I have disassociated from my feelings. I don't want to inhabit myself. I have nothing to live for.
- I am cut off from myself as well as from others.
- I feel alien in the world. I don't receive affection, and I don't give affection. I'm so lonely. I'm so unloved.

> *"If you meet a loner, no matter what they tell you,*
> *it's not because they enjoy solitude.*
> *It's because they have tried to blend into the world before,*
> *and people continue to disappoint them."*
> Jodi Picoult

- I am **out of touch with my emotions**. I don't feel them if I can help it. When I do feel some emotion, I don't know what it means. I don't trust feelings. I

    don't recognise or relate to others' feelings.
- I shame others for their passion and their childish play.
- I'm emotionally numb and live in an unfeeling way. I have difficulty expressing my emotions and have a very restricted emotional range.
- I see feeling as far less important than thinking. For me, they are an annoying impediment, inappropriate for a strong adult man.
- Despite restricting my emotions, I am often overcome with moods and inner anguish. Deep inside, mostly hidden from me, I am angst-ridden and emotionally turbulent.

> *"I could feel the tears brimming and sloshing in me*
> *like water in a glass*
> *that is unsteady and too full."*
> Sylvia Plath

- **I refuse to be vulnerable**, look silly, expose myself, or take off my armour.
- I make sure I am never vulnerable by withholding myself. I won't be spontaneous or let go and enjoy myself.
- I am hiding because I don't believe I am lovable or that anyone could love me.
- I won't let myself be hurt again. I won't show you how much I need you.
- I am rigid and afraid of change and fearful of new interpersonal situations. I don't want to risk engaging in new activities that may prove embarrassing to me.

"The humiliations he suffered when he first went to school had caused in him

a shrinking from his fellows which he could never entirely overcome;

he remained shy and silent.

But though he did everything to alienate the sympathy of other boys

he longed with all his heart for the popularity

which to some was so easily accorded.

These from his distance he admired extravagantly;

and though he was inclined to be more sarcastic with them than with others,

though he made little jokes at their expense,

he would have given anything to change places with them."

W. Somerset Maugham

- I am not connected to my **body**. I feel stiff, cold, old, brittle and fragile.
- I lack bodily feeling. I am out of touch with nature, with the earth.
- I have little touch in my life. I am not connected to others. I create very few opportunities to give and receive.
- I am afraid of getting old, of my body breaking down. I do not know what my body needs.

"Depression is the most unpleasant thing I have ever experienced. . . .
It is that absence of being able to envisage
that you will ever be cheerful again.
The absence of hope.
That very deadened feeling, which is so very different from feeling sad.
Sad hurts but it's a healthy feeling. It is a necessary thing to feel.
Depression is very different."
J.K. Rowling

- I'm **depressed**. Nothing works for me. There is no point in trying. It's all shit. I'm broken.
- I am **sad**. I am melancholy.

- I have trouble sleeping and struggle to get up in the morning.
- I am bored and have no capacity for delight. I lack enthusiasm.
- I'm **empty**, stuck, isolated, resigned, apathetic, and pessimistic. I'm chronically undercharged. I'm listless. I have too little energy and no zest or enthusiasm for life.
- I'm sad about what happened. Why did they leave? Was it me? I miss them so much. I so want them back. I'm so lonely.

"When you are irritable and paranoid and humourless and lifeless and critical and demanding and no reassurance is ever enough.
You're frightened, and you're frightening,
and you're "not at all like yourself but will be soon,
" but you know you won't."
Kay Redfield Jamison

The Lonely Lover Speaks

Each paragraph is the voice of a different man.

"I love from a distance. I am a hands-off lover."

"The Safety Officer controls me. My love is conditional. My giving and receiving are like issuing an invoice. I let myself get a little close, but not close enough so that they can get me. My love is scarce. I don't allow my heart to be broken or to open and grow. I never let myself fully commit to a relationship. And when I don't fully commit, that confirms to me that I am shit at relationships. In relationships, I am still holding on to the caterpillar so that I do not let the butterfly out. I stay out of relationships because I get overwhelmed by the feminine, I get in over my head. I lose myself.
I don't trust myself when I am involved with someone else.
I won't ever go after someone else. They have to come after me."

"I'm not sure, but I think I'm happy. I come out now and again. I don't feel free to express myself. My mother didn't like me crying. So I don't cry.
I moved away from it so my mother wouldn't be upset."

"I feel such grief that I've stopped myself from receiving. I've positioned myself not to trust the world. To stop love coming in. When it does, I feel such a sense of loss that I don't have that for myself."

"I don't know what to do. I feel sick. I can't feel anything. I can't read words. I'm so sad. I go silent. I am out of breath. I feel sick with it. It's too much for me to handle. I can't say anything. I can't stand out. I am restrained, asleep, acting dead."

"I want to fuck women and run away. I want to run away before any connection develops. A long-term relationship is too long, too scary. I go before I end up showing the darker parts of myself. It's too much. I run away from strong feelings. I'm always ready to run away. I can't help running away."

"Nobody is with me. I need someone physically. I am always alone. I'm not able to be a friend. I'm selfish. I always focus on my problems. I'm selfish and needy. I always think of myself. It's difficult to think about others. This is why I am alone. I focus on myself.
I don't see that others have problems. I'm really selfish and absorbed. I always complain about everything. I'm depressed, and no one can be my friend."

"I'm trapped. I'm so small. I am very frightened. The world is too much. It is overwhelming. The loneliness is crushing me."

"I pull away, I withdraw. I am uncomfortable. I avoid. I'm irritated, annoyed. I've got no flow. It's stuck under my ribs. Fuck off, leave me alone. Don't come to me. Let me figure it out on my own. Leave me alone."

"I don't like anyone. I'm suspicious of people. I avoid people. I pretend to be superior. I hate humanity. Humans are the cancer of the world. I protect myself from trauma, abuse, bullying. I am very scared of people. I am very shy. I am always angry with people. I push people away."

"I have to be good at it because if I am not, that proves I am unlovable. I listen out for how she thinks I am wrong. I blame myself. I try to plan ahead how I can get it right, so that she will love me. I plan so much I am not with her in the present at all."

"I can't feel. I try to feel it in my body. I do not know it. I am afraid of being engulfed. Maybe I can feel it in my head. Sometimes I can feel a little, and then I close up again."

"Life is too much. I want to numb out. I want to sleep. I just want to be comfortable. I am exhausted relating to people. I don't want to connect. People are too much. I don't want to get entangled. I get entangled too quickly. I want this to stop. I want isolation. Video games, tv."

At Times my Lover feels Sad

THE WELL OF GRIEF

"Those who will not slip beneath
the still surface on the well of grief,
turning down through its black water
to the place we cannot breathe,
will never know the source from which we drink,
the secret water, cold and clear,
nor find in the darkness glimmering,
the small round coins,
thrown by those who wished for something else."

David Whyte

Love holds one side of the coin of relationship, and grief holds the other. Grief is a part of love, and to love means accepting the possibility of loss. If I am afraid of the pain and anguish of sadness, I am not genuinely open to love. The degree to which I numb myself to sorrow is the degree to which I numb my whole emotional life. Love and grief are dual aspects of life, the tenderness and passion of love, the pain and anguish of grief.

"Any fool can be happy.
It takes a man with real heart to make beauty
out of the stuff that makes us weep".

Clive Barker

To freely mourn, I need a safe space. I need to take a step back from life to create a sacred space where I can let go of some of the things that need to be done, of my responsibilities for a time. Maybe, if I am lucky, I will have someone who can support me in my grieving, who can sit with me as I grieve, even when my grief seems overwhelming and unstoppable.

When I lose something or someone I love, I suffer from that loss. I carry the pain of the loss inside myself, and it hurts. My tears and my mourning acknowledge this loss, feel it, inhabit it and slowly release it. Feeling my grief returns me to fluid-flowing life. Painful grief is life-giving and rejuvenating, even as I feel my heart breaking.

If I do not grieve, my sadness and loss congeal and solidify. It lodges deep inside me, a cold, buried, unacknowledged frozen waste. When I cannot cry, I fail to acknowledge what I have lost, and I do not mourn its passing.

Just because I don't grieve doesn't mean that I have disconnected from my loss. It just means that I stay connected to what or whom I have lost in a painful, rigid manner. If I don't attend to my pain and never tend to my grief, I remember in pain and never move to celebrate the person I lost.

Loss demands that I mourn, and then in time, I can move on. Grief needs tears to soften it, bring acceptance, restore flow, and enhance and reignite my connection to life. I mourn, and I honour what I have lost. In time I celebrate what I had so that I connect to my loss in a joyful rather than painful way.

> *"You cannot protect yourself from sadness without protecting yourself from happiness".*
> Jonathan Safran Foer

Sadness is honest, and it demands my involvement. With my tears, I settle, release toxins and pain, and move on, lighter and more connected. As I move through grief, I am not trying to "get rid of it". I am learning to live with the pain inherent in life. By mourning, I move deeper into life, knowing that I can accept and move through pain and loss.

In her book 'On Death and Dying', Elisabeth Kubler-Ross states that grieving often has five stages and that we spend varying times in them and feel shifting intensity of emotion in each stage. We may not go through them in any particular order, and we may not go through every stage, but they are a valuable way of looking at how we grieve.

1). Denying what has happened.

When we first face the loss of a loved one, it is so hard to accept. It is normal for us to react with disbelief and say no to what has happened. This reaction is part of our defence mechanism, and it helps us cope with the immediate shock. We may find ourselves wanting to block out what has happened. We may want to step away from the world and isolate ourselves, to find a way to cope, and give ourselves time to face up to our loss.

2). Becoming Angry.

We may struggle to come out of denial to face what has happened and work out how we will manage. At this stage, it is normal to feel anger. Anger steps up when we are not ready to accept the depths of our pain and loss. We direct ourselves away from our vulnerable sadness and express anger instead. This is particularly the case for us men who are comfortable with anger and uncomfortable with sadness. So, instead of feeling sad, we explode in anger, perhaps at inanimate objects or at the people around us. Maybe we feel angry with health professionals, who we judge have not done enough. We may even feel angry with the one we have lost. We feel mad at them for leaving us or for the way they left us. Our anger can be confusing, especially if we don't want to feel angry with the person we love. These conflicting emotions are especially complicated when we lose someone to suicide.

3). Trying to Bargain

We may try to make a deal with God or our higher power to change the outcome. When we are faced with a situation, we can't change, this is a typical reaction. We may criticise ourselves for not doing more or for not creating a different outcome. We bargain to put off the inevitable and to postpone facing up to it.

4). Depression - sinking into Mourning

Profound loss can fundamentally change our world. This loss, and the change it brings, takes time to acclimatise to, accept, and mourn. It is tough to face and deal with all the practical matters that surface when someone dies or when our relationship breaks down. When those matters have been taken care of, we may be left lonely and alone, on our own, facing our new life without the one we love.

5. Acceptance

At this stage, which we may not reach, we make our terms and accept what has happened. It's not easy to get here, and we might resist if we feel we are betraying our lost loved one by accepting their absence and our loss.

Here we finally make peace and seek to re-engage with life.

Your process through grieving may look pretty different to this, but hopefully, these five steps will give you some idea of what you will face.

> "If we are strong enough to be weak enough,
> we are given a wound that never heals.
> It is the gift that keeps the heart open."
> Oriah Mountain Dreamer

Unhealthy Sadness – Too Much and Too Little

As with all these archetypal human processes, when we struggle to engage with them, we end up living either too much of the archetype or too little. I have listed the behaviours of each so you can spot where you sit on the sadness spectrum and try to adjust your approach.

Behaviours showing up with Too Much Sadness

- Being submerged in despair that does not change, move or reach a resolution.
- Feeling sad when we need to be angry.
- Experiencing physical problems such as loss of strength and stamina, loss of appetite, shortness of breath, and unspecific physical pain around your heart.
- Being full of despair, hopelessness, and despondency.
- Becoming imprisoned by sadness so that you cannot flow or move with it.
- Being crushed by sorrow so that you feel life has no point and you cannot function in the world.
- Being very soft or passive and over-attentive to others.
- Not being well defined, having no boundaries, and failing to protect yourself.
- Refusing to move on and identifying with being 'the wronged one' or 'the wounded one'.
- Being locked in a despairing drama and not allowing anything to relieve your anguish.

- <u>Behaviours showing up with Too Little Sadness</u>
- Feeling stuck, dry and arid.
- Being inflexible and lacking in flow.
- Being constantly angry while not being able to be sad.
- Saying you are 'okay' when you are not. Pretending you are happy.
- Refusing to face your sadness by shifting attention away from yourself and changing the subject.
- Ignoring your pain while focusing on others' pain.
- Blocking or ignoring your sadness, keeping it in place, and not allowing rejuvenation or healing.
- Not being able to be with others' sadness in case it touches your grief.
- Losing touch with all your lover attributes.
- Being unable to feel any of your emotions.
- Losing touch with your body.

A Process to Support You Being Sad

In this process, you have an opportunity to 'tend to your grief'. Here you will feel into and remember when you lost someone or something that you love and value.

We will be using the Five Stages of Grief from Francis Weller's book 'The Wild Edge of Sorrow'. We will spend time at each gate.

You will feel and witness your grief so that you can release it into your Sovereign healing, love and acceptance.

To go onto such a vulnerable place, you need to feel safe, so set aside a particular time for this process. Check to make sure that you will not be disturbed. Create a secure and protected physical space where you are safe.

Gate One:

> 'Tis a fearful thing to love what death can touch.
> A fearful thing to love, to hope, to dream, to be –
> to be, and oh, to lose.
> A thing for fools, this, and a holy thing,
> a holy thing to love.
> For your life has lived in me,
> your laugh once lifted me,
> your word was a gift to me.
> To remember this brings painful joy.
> 'Tis a human thing, love,
> a holy thing, to love what death has touched."
> Yehuda Halevi

Everything we love, we lose. Feel into who or what you have lost. Remember that person or place and bring to mind how it felt to be with them, how much love and joy you felt. Sense how much you miss them. Mourn for them.

Gate Two:

'The Places That Have Not Known Love'

'There are places in us that that have been wrapped in shame and banished to the farthest shores of our lives'.

Dear King, what places in you have not felt your love? What parts of yourself are you ashamed of so that you hide them and banish them from your heart?

When you get a sense of a part of you calling for your love and inclusion, go to that part. Hold and love that part, just as you know best. Feel how it was for that part of you to be banished from your heart-full home. Sympathise and empathise with this part of you. Love this part of you and bring it into your heart.

Gate Three:

'The Sorrows of the World'

'The cumulative grief of the world is overwhelming'.

There is so much grief in the world as we start to see what we are doing to our earthly home—all the loss of so many species we used to share our planet with. Our world is heating up. Will we even survive? What will happen to our children and our grandchildren? Let yourself grieve this vast loss.

Gate Four:

'What We Expected and Did Not Receive'.

What broke your heart as a child? What happened when you expected to receive love and were given something else? Feel into the losses you faced as a child when your hope of love and holding did not happen. Feel the sorrow in your inner boy.

And how has your adult life turned out? Have you been able to create the life you want? Have you been able to offer your unique gifts to the world? Feel the sorrow of any of your unlived life?

Gate Five:

'Ancestral Grief'

We carry within us the residue of grief from the sorrow, loss and disappointments of our ancestors. We are the living evolution of a long line of men and women. In many cases, their lives were extremely harsh and challenging. Their essence runs through our make-up. What of their grief and sorrow can you cry out? What runs down your family line that you can grieve and bring resolution to?

> '*Sorrow prepares you for Joy.*
> *It violently sweeps everything out of your house,*
> *so that new joy can find space to enter.*
> *It shakes the yellow leaves from the bough of your heart,*
> *so that fresh, green leaves can grow in their place.*
> *It pulls up the rotten roots,*
> *so that new roots hidden beneath have room to grow.*
> *Whatever sorrow shakes from your heart,*
> *far better things will take their place!*'
> Rumi

How was it for you to deliberately spend time with your sadness, to mourn? You may want to do this process several times, with the same loss or with different losses. While it is painful to spend time grieving, it is also revitalising. Tending to our pain rather than ignoring it means that we give value to what we have lost.

> "When it's time to suffer, you should suffer;
> when it's time to cry, you should cry.
> Cry completely.
> Cry until there are no more tears
> and then recognise in your exhaustion that you're alive.
> The sun still rises and sets.
> The seasons come and go.
> Absolutely nothing remains the same,
> and that includes suffering.
> When the suffering ends,
> wisdom begins to raise the right questions."
> Seido Ray Ronci

Part 6

Conclusion and Next Steps

The Sovereign's Journey is a spiral, a circling around our inner world, our internal character. Our Heart King seeks to know us and this process if one of deepening, moving more into ourselves, gradually realising more and more about who we are. It is a life journey, rather than a fixed road with a definite destination.

Every time I see myself functioning in a particular archetype, I realise more about myself. Every time I consider an archetype, or I work with an archetype with other me, I realise more about myself. This is an ongoing Journey.

If you would like to join with me, and with other men on our Sovereign's Journey, there are several ways you can do this.

Join The Sovereign's Journey group on Facebook. Here we continually explore the different archetypes in this book.

Join me on one of my free Zoom workshops where you will have a chance to embody the archetype we are currently working on. Email me if you want to join at hpnewton@hotmail.co.uk

Join myself or Geof for 1 to 1 deep personal work. Email me your details to work with either of us.

Join me on retreat where you will establish and build your Heart King, allay with the forces of creation that support you, and where your Heart King will get to know and make terms with all the archetypal figures inside. Below are outlines of the retreats that make up The Sovereign's Journey. Have a look at the website where you can see an outline of the retreats: - https://www.thesovereignsjourney.co.uk/retreats

I bless you if you have made it to the end of this book. I know it is a beautiful, and at times painful journey. I bless your courage and your willingness to grow and become whole.

I hope to see you at some time and join with you on The Sovereign's Journey.

With love from Hugh.

Appendix 1
What is Trauma, and how does it Affects You?

"Traumatic events, by definition, overwhelm our ability to cope.
When the mind becomes flooded with emotion,
a circuit breaker is thrown that allows us to survive the experience fairly intact,
that is, without becoming psychotic or frying out one of the brain centres.
The cost of this blown circuit is emotion frozen within the body.
In other words, we often unconsciously stop feeling our trauma partway into it,
like a movie that is still going after the sound has been turned off.
We cannot heal until we move fully through that trauma,
including all the feelings of the event."

Susan Pease Banitt

The word trauma comes from the Greek word for wound.

We can be wounded by violence or by the threat of violence. We can be traumatised by being injured ourselves or by witnessing others being threatened or hurt. A traumatic incident may overwhelm our ability to cope and leave us feeling helpless, out of control, full of horror and terror, and afraid of being hurt or annihilated. Post-Traumatic Stress Disorder (PTSD) is the term used for how this wounding affects us.

Trauma can come from one or more horrible events that are so awful that anyone would be affected. It may also come from less severe events which affect some people but not others.

"Traumatised people chronically feel unsafe inside their bodies:
The past is alive in the form of gnawing interior discomfort.
Their bodies are constantly bombarded by visceral warning signs,
and, in an attempt to control these processes,
they often become expert at ignoring their gut feelings
and in numbing awareness of what is played out inside.
They learn to hide from their selves."

Bessel A. van der Kolk

There is a normal human reaction to catastrophe. When we are threatened, our sympathetic nervous system arouses us with Adrenalin, so we become fully alert. Our nervous system brings us to a place of very focused attention on our immediate situation so that we can react strongly to save ourselves and, if necessary, ignore our pain and exhaustion to stay alive. We have been mobilised to fight or fly. Our emotions are aroused to intense fear or anger, our attention is utterly focused, and our perceptions are sharp and clear. We work at this level to achieve safety as soon as possible.

When something awful happens, we are profoundly shocked. This shock reverberates through our body and mind. It is like an alarm bell ringing in our system. We return to its urgent call again and again. We return to reassure ourselves that it's not happening now and that we are safe. We also revisit because we have been injured by what happened. While our physical injuries may have mostly healed, the psychological harm also needs to be attended to. Our internal system wants us to find some way of coming to terms with what happened and heal our psychic wound.

> "Some scars don't hurt. Some scars are numb.
> Some scars rid you of the capacity to feel anything."
> Joyce Rachelle

Trauma can break up the links between our previously integrated functions. We may end up remembering the traumatic event in precise detail while having no emotions about it. We may experience deep emotions and not be able to recognise what produced them. Traumatic symptoms often become disconnected from the event that caused them. They start to take on a life of their own.

Trauma causes fragmentation, so we struggle to integrate what happened to us. Our traumatic memory may end up set apart from our everyday consciousness. As Abram Kardiner described, *"the whole apparatus for concerted, coordinated and purposeful activity is smashed"*. Our perceptions become inaccurate, and fear saturates our life. Our judgements turn out to be skewed, and we can't make sense of our world. We respond to ordinary situations with anger and aggression, or we numb out and detach, so we don't respond at all.

> "Dissociation gets you through a brutal experience,
> letting your basic survival skills operate unimpeded…
> Your ability to survive is enhanced as the ability to feel is diminished…
> All feeling are blocked; you 'go away.'
> You are disconnected from the act, the perpetrator & yourself…
> Viewing the scene from up above or some other out-of-body perspective
> is common among sexual abuse survivors."
> Renee Fredrickson

Complex PTSD

Another form of PTSD has been recognised. Complex PTSD occurs when we are subject to ongoing traumatic events repeated for an extended time. If we cannot get away from ongoing trauma, especially in childhood, we will be more deeply traumatised. We may have been trapped in a traumatic environment for some time. We become traumatised when security is not available, when no escape is possible, and when we have to stay at this heightened level for more extended periods. This can mean that, even when we are out of danger and no longer under threat, we continue to respond as if we were still in danger. The trauma we faced profoundly changed our psychological memory, emotions, thought process, and arousal levels. Because of this, we end up feeling deeply distrustful towards the world, empty and hopeless, permanently damaged and different from everyone else.

> "When the black thing was at its worst,
> when the illicit cocktails and the ten-mile runs stopped working,
> I would feel numb as if dead to the world.
> I moved unconsciously, with heavy limbs, like a zombie from a horror film.
> I felt a pain so fierce and persistent deep inside me,
> I was tempted to take the chopping knife in the kitchen and cut the black thing out.
> I would lie on my bed staring at the ceiling thinking about that knife and using all my limited
> powers of self-control to stop myself from going downstairs to get it."
>
> Alice Jamieson

Trauma experienced in childhood has a powerful effect. Traumatic difficulties in childhood are called Adverse Childhood Experiences (ACE). The more ACE's we suffer from in childhood, the more likely our healthy development is damaged. As a result, we are more likely we are to suffer from unhealthy trauma-related behaviours in adulthood. Childhood trauma is exacerbated by Attachment Trauma which results when a child cannot attach to his parents in a 'good enough' way.

Whether we experience trauma as a child or an adult, we have to manage its effects. We may experience general symptoms such as anger and anxiety. We may also experience specific symptoms that are 'triggered' when we find ourselves in a situation that reminds us of the traumatic events that wounded us.

Sadly, having experienced trauma, we may also encounter its consequences, which include:

- Excessive fear, which leads us to try to hide from the world and from our symptoms. We may go numb, detach, and disassociate. We may run away from difficult situations and become anxious, afraid and isolated. We find that we startle easily, are hyper-alert, over-vigilant, and suffer from poor sleep and nightmares.

- High levels of sadness. A traumatic event might involve profound loss and betrayal. The pain from these continues to hurt us as it churns around inside so that we may feel lost, upset and depressed. To survive this sadness, we may try to get away from it with drugs or alcohol. We may swing from feeling overwhelmingly sad to feeling nothing at all.

- Endless churning anger. We may feel angry about what happened, or our anger and rage may rise to defend us. The trauma may lead us to lash out, especially when we are 'triggered'. We may be violent ourselves, threatening, and aggressive in challenging situations.

- Self-criticism and self-judgement. We may believe the trauma was our fault and that we should have been able to prevent it. Our self-punishing may include hurting ourselves physically or with drugs, alcohol, food, or damaging relationships. Flashbacks may exacerbate this, or we may find ourselves re-enacting the trauma without realising it.

- Physical trauma. Our physical system is disordered by trauma, so we may suffer from health issues, disease, psychosomatic illnesses, and long-term ailments that degrade our life experience.

> "Some people with DID present their narratives of sadistic abuse
> in a quite matter-of-fact way, without perceptible affect.
> This may sometimes be done as a way of protecting themselves,
> and the listener, from the emotional impact of their experience.
> We have found that people describing trauma in a flat way,
> without feeling, are usually those who have been more chronically abused, while those with affect still have a sense of self that can observe
> the tragedy of betrayal and have feelings about it."
> Graeme Galton

<u>Healing from Trauma</u>

> "There is no timestamp on trauma.
> There isn't a formula that you can insert yourself into
> to get from horror to healed.
> Be patient. Take up space.
> Let your journey be the balm."
> Dawn Serra

It is possible to heal from trauma. How long this takes depends on the age you experienced the trauma, how awful it was, and how long it lasted. If you were very young and it lasted a long time, it will take a longer time to heal.

> "The big issue for traumatised people is that
> they don't own themselves anymore.
> Any loud sound, anybody insulting them, hurting them, saying bad things,
> can hijack them away from themselves.
> And so what we have learned is that what makes you resilient to trauma
> is to own yourself fully."
> Dr. Bessel Van Der Kolk

In this book, you will be spending a lot of time with parts of yourself that have experienced trauma. To work with trauma needs great care. It needs to be done in an atmosphere of safety and trust. We cannot do this work here in the book, but on our retreats, your Heart King will have multiple opportunities to know and care for the parts of you that experienced trauma.

In safety, your King will help these parts of you come to terms with what happened and make an acceptable story of it. You will see that your trauma is a part of you, not all of you. Your King will be able to love and support the wounded parts of you, assuring them that they were not to blame. He will hold and defend your wounded aspects so that you are held, safe and loved. He will manage your reaction to your trauma and will slowly regulate your behaviour.

> "To heal is to touch with love that which we previously touched with fear."
> Stephen Levine

In time your King will support you to see what meaning this trauma has for you. He will show you what you have learned and how to build value and purpose from it. He will help you integrate and grow from your past difficulties. In time your King will create a strong, inclusive, loving heart filled home for your traumatised parts so that you can move forward and build the beautiful life you choose.

> "Trauma often shatters belief systems and robs people
> of their sense of meaning.
> In so doing, it forces people to put the pieces back together...
> rebuilding beautifully those parts of their lives and life stories
> that they could never have torn down voluntarily."
> Jonathan Haidt

Appendix 2
Exercises for each Archetype

Heart Sovereign

Strengthening your King

Our Heart King provides us with an outline of ourselves at our best. We may not always be able to live as our Heart King, but awareness of ourselves in this beautiful Archetypes gives us something to aim for, especially when our Healthy King falls of our throne and is replaced by some other part.

Having read through the outline decide on the behaviours, beliefs and outlook of your Heart King. Write these up into a number of bullet points.

This is now your outline of yourself in your Heart King archetype.

If you want to strengthen your King then take some time each morning to meditate on and enhance this part of yourself. You can look at yourself in the mirror and repeat your King's lines. Doing this you keep your attention on your King, and keep your Sovereign on your throne as your day progresses.

Watching your Magician's Thoughts

It is important for your Sovereign to separate himself from his Magician. Your Sovereign wants to establish himself as the one who watches his thoughts, but not the one who is doing the thinking.

Clever Magician

Watching your Fear

Our Magician lets us know when we may be in a challenging situation through fear. When you work on Retreat with your Safety Officer you will regulate the levels of fear in your system. Until then you can watch out for how much fear you are feeling in your life, and when your fear comes up. Notice how strong your fear is and what effect it has on you. Get used to the idea that you do not have to give in to your fear, but that your Sovereign can interrogate it to make sense of what difficulty or threat he is facing.

Watching your Inner Critic and the Shame you feel

It is very useful for your Sovereign to become very aware of how your Inner Critic operates, and the level of shame that this part administers. You will be working with this on Retreat, but in the meantime, it is helpful for you to watch and get to know how and when this part of you operates.

Strong Warrior

Being Strong

Knowing that your Warrior holds your sense of self and your personal power, what can you do to build your strong egoic base? Notice when your Warrior is successful and accomplishes things for you. Thank and praise your Warrior to build your sense of self.

Expressing Appropriate Anger

Get clear on your relationship with your anger. Does your anger flow easily and strongly, or do you repress your anger until it bursts out. Get used to expressing anger as a muscle.

Managing your Boundaries

How are your boundaries. It is useful to notice where you hold clear recognisable boundaries, and where you enforce them too strongly. Notice also who walks over your boundaries, and your reaction to that.

Connected Lover

Grief and Sadness

How much access do you have to grief and sadness? Being able to grieve is so important for our internal feeling health system, but our culture discourages strong feelings, particularly sadness and tears. Notice how easy it is for you to cry, and notice what comes up to block your feeling and expressions of sadness.

What parts of you discourage Connection

Our Lover is a place where many of us got hurt early in life, especially if we grew up in a more Patriarchal society. Because of this we may have learned to suppress our feelings and our need for loving connection.

Watch out for the parts of yourself that try to suppress your feelings and your need to connect to others. How do these parts block you or shut you down?

Printed in Great Britain
by Amazon